THE
Signers
of the
Declaration
of
Independence

THE
SIGNERS
OF THE
DECLARATION
OF
INDEPENDENCE

Brother C. Edward Quinn, FSC

872884

THE BRONX COUNTY HISTORICAL SOCIETY
THE BRONX, NEW YORK

ISBN 0-941980-20-0

THE BRONX COUNTY HISTORICAL SOCIETY
3309 Bainbridge Avenue, The Bronx, New York 10467

Editors

Gary D. Hermalyn
Lloyd Ultan

Cover and Book Design by
Henry C. Meyer Jr.

TABLE OF CONTENTS

ACKNOWLEDGMENTS

I am grateful to Dr. Theodore E. B. Wood of the Educational Consortium of America, for having started me on the previous book of life sketches of the signers of the Declaration of Independence. He was an encouraging editor, and I appreciate his help in getting the original version of this book into print. The incentive to do an expanded version has come largely from Mr. Robert R. Hall, President, and Dr. Gary D. Hermalyn, Executive Director, of The Bronx County Historical Society. Both removed obstacles and prodded the author into action. I owe sincere thanks also to Professor Lloyd Ultan of Fairleigh Dickinson University for his comments and suggestions, both witty and perceptive.

Invaluable help came, as it always does, from the staff of The Bronx County Historical Society. My thanks to Mr. Jeremy Geller, Ms. Mary Ilario, Mrs. Laura Tosi and Mrs. Kay Gleeson. Their ability to do so much constantly amazes me. I am happy to dedicate this work to them as a tribute to their skillful and energetic, if largely unsung, contribution to the cause of good history.

Brother C. Edward Quinn

PREFACE TO THE SECOND EDITION

The excitement generated by the 1987 Constitution Bicentennial unquestionably reawakened interest in the events that had preceded the formulation of our national charter. Of these occurrences, surely the most notable were the vote for separation from Great Britain and the proclamation of the Declaration of Independence.

Reconsidering the Declaration in the light of the Constitution has reinforced my admiration of the earlier document, and prompted me to look once more at my earlier book on the signers of 1776. In that volume, I attempted to present thumbnail biographies, or character sketches, of the fifty-six signers of Thomas Jefferson's trumpet call to freedom.

Could there ever have been the concise, coolly phrased Constitution if there had not been the dramatic Declaration? Would there have been any opportunity to form a stable government if an earlier group had not proclaimed the freedom that the Constitution would preserve? Which group was greater, the rebels who defied the British hangman or the statesmen who made liberty enduring? The question is rhetorical, of course; if either group had not played its role, if either had faltered, we would have had no occasion to celebrate either bicentennial. From the perspective of two centuries, we can plainly see that the Declaration signers had to dare before the Constitution framers could establish.

Although there was some interaction and overlap between these two sets of Founding Fathers, there was less than might have been expected. For one thing, only six men signed both documents, although the time between them was a mere eleven years. Roger Sherman of Connecticut; Benjamin Franklin, James Wilson, Robert Morris, and George Clymer of Pennsylvania; and George Read of Delaware were the sole signatories to both charters. Furthermore, only two other signers of the Declaration, Elbridge Gerry of Massachusetts and George Wythe of Virginia, even attended the Constitutional Convention. Gerry did not like the final document and refused to sign it; Wythe lost his chance when he returned to Virginia to be with his ailing wife. One Constitution signer, John Dickinson of Delaware, had earlier refused to sign the Declaration. There would have been a few more Declaration signers at the Convention, but some who were elected delegates declined to attend. For example, Richard Henry Lee, Abraham Clark, and Thomas Stone did not go to Philadelphia, the latter two because of illness, and Lee because he feared the Convention might indeed write a Constitution that would diminish the power of the individual states.

There were a few cases of close relatives involved in the signings. Charles Carroll of Carrollton, a Declaration signer, was a first cousin of Constitution signer Daniel Carroll. Declaration signer Lewis Morris was the half-brother of Constitution signer Gouverneur Morris. Edward Rutledge (Declaration) was a younger brother of John Rutledge (Constitution), and Philip Livingston (Declaration) was an older brother of William Livingston (Constitution). Yet despite these interconnections, the two sets of signers remain decidedly distinct.

There was also a significant difference in the manner of signing the two documents. The Constitution was signed by the Convention delegates present who were willing to acknowledge that the document represented "the unanimous consent of the States present." Forty-two of these were on hand in Philadelphia on September 17, 1787, and all but three signed. In the case of the Declaration of Independence, Congressional delegates were continually arriving and departing. Some were present during the independence debate July 2-4; others were not. Some who were not there signed afterward; others did not. Some sensed that their signatures assured them niches among history's immortals; others were too busy with state or personal matters to notice.

The Appendix lists the eligible Congressional delegates who did not sign, as well as those signers elected between July 4 and the actual date of the signing. Although printed copies of the text of the Declaration were ready as early as July 5, the formal document itself, painstakingly inscribed by hand on parchment, was not presented for signatures until August 2. Members of Congress present on that day signed, including those not present for the independence debates. Some delegates, absent on August 2, signed whenever they next arrived in Philadelphia; others did not bother at all, even though they could indeed have done so. There is, therefore, a touch of the haphazard about the fifty-six actual signatories. An attempt is made in the appendix to explain why delegates who could have signed did not. In some cases, their reasons are perfectly clear; in others, they either did not return to Philadelphia at all, or, if they did, they gave little thought to the meaning their signatures would have for future generations.

It may seem odd that celebrating the Constitution should

demonstrate again that the Declaration has lost none of its appeal. Yet how could it? Jefferson's glowing prose, flowing and rhythmic, still throbs with the pulse of freedom's quest. It is high drama on parchment, and its signers are dramatic figures who shared in a bright moment that blazed up into the American Revolution and victory at Yorktown. The Constitution signers also gave off light, but theirs was more subdued, the steady gleam of the lamp on the desk; they were the planners rather than the bold proclaimers.

Upon rereading my original sketches for the 1975 publication of the Declaration signers, I found little that I wished to change. However, some features have been added. The text of the Declaration is included, and there are lists of those present in Congress July 2-4, the members of Congress at that time who never signed, the signers who were not members of Congress July 2-4, those signers who were members of Congress, but were absent July 2-4, and those who signed later than August 2. Also included are a brief description of the committee appointed June 11 to draft the Declaration, a summary of some precursors of the Declaration of Independence, the text of the Lee Resolutions proposing independence, some information on the graves of the signers, and a bibliography.

In addition, the order of sketches is presented in geographical sequence from north to south, New Hampshire to Georgia, in the order in which the states' delegates actually signed. The illustrations are taken from the work by William H. Michael listed in the bibliography at the back of this book.

I hope that this expanded version will prove useful, interesting, and enjoyable. I also hope that it may furnish some basis for comparing the two sets of Founding Fathers. As individuals they probably did not differ much from each other, but the roles they played stand out in sharp contrast. As deserving of our admiration as the Constitution framers surely are, they would not have been needed without their predecessors of 1776. It was this earlier group who, to paraphrase Harry Truman, took the heat as they stood in the sweltering kitchen of the American Revolution. The products of the labors of both groups, the two documents on which our national heritage rests today, as it always has, now repose under reverent protection in the National Archives in Washington.

INTRODUCTION

The signers of the Declaration of Independence demonstrated rare courage and foresight in consenting to a document that made them traitors to the British Crown. We know now that their courage paid handsome dividends, but at the time it was a leap in the dark, sustained only by heroic faith in the future of America.

Robert Morris took this leap when he backed Congress's valueless currency with his own credit in a desperate effort to avert national bankruptcy. His subsequent financial collapse cost him three years in a debtors' prison. Benjamin Harrison and Carter Braxton also took this leap. As custodians of proud heritages, they were dedicated to preserving and transmitting family wealth and prestige. But safeguarding inheritances demanded precisely the kind of attention to private matters that these leaders could not give. Occupied with the business of the struggling nation, they watched helplessly as their estates shrank and the original objectives of their lives became unattainable.

Other men gambled their health. Thomas Nelson fatally aggravated his asthma in the service of America. Aristocrat Philip Livingston doggedly remained at his Congressional duties until death took him from his post in 1778. Sickly Joseph Hewes died of overwork in 1779. Especially moving is the case of Caesar Rodney, afflicted with cancer and knowing that his name on the Declaration removed any chance for help at the hands of British surgeons.

Some signers lost their liberty as a result of participating in the Revolution. Richard Stockton was imprisoned in 1776, treated harshly, and released a dying man. George Walton was captured at Savannah in 1778. Edward Rutledge, Thomas Heyward, and Arthur Middleton were taken at Charleston in 1780.

One of the Revolution's most poignant tragedies involved Benjamin Franklin and his son William, the last Royal Governor of

New Jersey. Close confidants in happier days, Franklin and his son parted forever on the question of independence, each going to his grave convinced the other was a traitor.

The mutual pledging of lives, fortunes, and honor was no mere rhetoric. The signers risked, and often lost, wealth, health, and personal liberty in affirming the high value they placed on human freedom.

JOHN HANCOCK
Massachusetts

January 12, 1737   *October 8, 1793*

President of the Congress

John Hancock, the son of a minister, was born in what is now Quincy, Massachusetts. The story of his bold signature on the Declaration of Independence (so that John Bull would not need his glasses to read it) is well known to almost everyone. But Hancock's contributions to American independence were much more substantial than that.

Orphaned as a boy, Hancock was adopted by his wealthy uncle

Thomas, a prominent merchant. The young man thus attained a leading place in Boston society and became deeply involved in the commerce of that city. When the movement for American independence gathered momentum in the 1760s Hancock was already influential. He joined other Massachusetts leaders in organizing vigorous demonstrations against the Stamp Act of 1775. So embittered did the Stamp Act leave Bostonians that, when Hancock's sloop *Liberty* was seized by the British on a smuggling charge, he found himself a hero in the eyes of his fellow citizens.

Hancock served in the Massachusetts Colonial legislature (the General Court as it was called then) and was active in nearly every phase of the independence movement, including the revolutionary Committee of Safety. The British so feared Hancock's ability to stir up rebellion that, when they offered a general pardon to the people of Massachusetts in June 1775, he and Sam Adams were specifically excluded. By that time, however, Hancock had reached Philadelphia and been elected President of the Continental Congress. Thus Hancock had the honor of presiding over the group of distinguished leaders who gave America the independence for which he had so long struggled.

A dedicated and generous supporter of independence, Hancock was at the same time conceited and touchy. Throughout his later life, he was tormented by gout, a painful disease that made his tendency to crankiness even more pronounced. Despite such human frailties, Hancock was repeatedly elected governor of Massachusetts after his service in Congress had ended. He died while governor and received the biggest funeral his state had ever seen. The feisty old patriot, always fond of display, would have loved it.

JOSIAH BARTLETT
New Hampshire

November 21, 1729   *May 19, 1795*

Josiah Bartlett, one of five physicians to sign the Declaration of Independence, illustrates an interesting point: eighteenth century American physicians were often extremely influential. Perhaps this was because people felt that a good doctor was genuinely interested in their welfare and merited their trust.

Was Josiah Bartlett this sort of doctor? Well, his only medical training was an apprenticeship to an established physician which ended when Bartlett felt he had acquired sufficient skill to go on his own. And go on his own he did! He once cured himself of a prolonged fever by consuming prodigious quantities of cider. That is certainly unconventional therapy. Less unorthodox was his use of quinine in treating sore throats. But the supreme tribute to Bartlett's qualities as a physician is surely the fact that three of his sons and seven of his grandsons followed him in the profession. He must have set quite an example for them.

In any case, Dr. Bartlett, born in Amesbury, Massachusetts, but by 1776 a resident of Kingston, New Hampshire, certainly had the confidence of his fellow citizens. They elected him to almost every office available, most notably to Congress and the governor's chair. It seems clear that he was regarded as both a skillful physician and a capable leader.

Bartlett is interesting in relation to the Declaration for a special reason. The signing was done in the geographical order of states from north to south. New Hampshire was the northernmost state and Bartlett its senior delegate. Therefore to him, after President of Congress John Hancock, went the honor of being the first to sign the great document. Such a distinction could not have been conferred on a more dedicated patriot.

Bartlett also stood at another crossroads of American history. At the Constitutional Convention of 1787 it was agreed that the Federal Constitution would become effective once it had been ratified by conventions in nine of the thirteen states. Eight states had ratified by the time the final vote came up in the New Hampshire convention. This much-admired statesman was a persuasive advocate of ratification and New Hampshire's favorable vote assuring a new national government was due in no small part to Bartlett's efforts. It was a fitting conclusion to his work as a Founding Father, begun about a dozen years before, when he had put his name to the Declaration itself.

WILLIAM WHIPPLE
New Hampshire

January 14, 1730   *November 10, 1785*

William Whipple's home has an unmistakable flavor of the sea as it looks out on Portsmouth harbor. It still has the railed-in "widow's walk" on the roof, and the old counting house is there too. Despite changes all around it, the old owner would instantly recognize these familiar features of his New England sea captain's home.

The house was originally built in 1763 for Whipple's father-in-law, Samuel Moffatt, but Whipple was a worthy inheritor of the stately residence. The signer had himself been a man of the sea in his youth, earning command of his own vessel while still in his twenties. After about ten years as a mariner, he settled down to the life of a landbound merchant, using his counting house as an office.

Despite his intimate connection with the sea, however, this Founding Father is usually known to history as General Whipple. The title refers to his command of New Hampshire troops at Saratoga and, later, near Newport, Rhode Island. At Saratoga he took part in the negotiations that ended in Burgoyne's surrender on October 17, 1777. There is a story that, before the battle began at Saratoga, General Whipple freed his slave in order to give him sufficient reason for fighting bravely.

After 1775, Whipple's life was entirely taken up with public service, civil and military. He was a member of Congress from 1776 to 1779, a member of the New Hampshire legislature after that, and a justice of the Supreme Court of his state from 1782 to 1785.

One aspect of Whipple's life merits special attention. As a sea captain he came into contact with the slave trade. In fact, he seems even to have acted as master of a slave ship. The brutality of this grim commerce sharpened his appreciation of the value of freedom to the human spirit. Not only did he liberate a slave of his own, but he devoted the last ten years of his life to building an America that would be both a symbol and a source of freedom to people everywhere.

This Founding Father died of heart disease at the age of 55. His dedication to the American cause and his contagious optimism about its ultimate success were two solid stones that he personally placed in the new nation's foundation.

MATTHEW THORNTON
New Hampshire

? 1714   *June 24, 1803*

Matthew Thornton, brought from Ireland by his parents about 1718, was by 1776 a seasoned veteran of New Hampshire politics. He first lived in Maine and later in Worcester, Massachusetts, where he served a medical apprenticeship. But after 1740 his entire professional and political career was spent in New Hampshire and among its people. In that year he began his medical practice in the small town of Londonderry.

During King George's War (1740-1748) he served in a New Hampshire regiment as its "under-surgeon," taking part in the successful assault on the French fort at Louisbourg, Canada, in 1745. From 1758 to 1775 Thornton was a member of the provincial legislature. By 1765, however, the future signer had developed serious reservations about British rule. These came to the fore when he led local agitation against the detested Stamp Act. He presided over the Provincial Congress in 1775 when the break with England became irreparable, and in 1776 was elected to the Second Continental Congress, taking his seat in November. He put his name to the Declaration then, months after most of the others had signed.

Thornton was an exceptionally durable man. After moving to Merrimack, New Hampshire in 1780, he served in the State Senate (1784-1786) while in his seventies. He undertook the preparation of a treatise called *Paradise Lost: or the Origin of the Evil Called Sin* while in his eighties, and even survived a bout with whooping cough as an octogenarian.

Matthew Thornton, it must be admitted, was a puzzling man. He was tall, dark-eyed, and impressive—everybody agreed on that; but opinions differed on some of his other qualities. Some thought him stingy; others praised him as a splendid host. Some found him sarcastic; others delighted in his sharp wit. Benjamin Rush spoke of Thornton as being given to telling stories "for the most part well chosen." What the Philadelphian apparently meant was that Thornton's humor was genuine enough, but occasionally a bit racy for the tastes of solemn folks.

Thornton died at 89 while visiting a daughter in Newburyport, Massachusetts. His sturdy physique had carried him unflinchingly through the trying years of America's birth and infancy. If not one of our best known Founding Fathers, he was certainly one of the most dedicated and industrious of them.

SAMUEL ADAMS
Massachusetts

September 27, 1722   *October 2, 1803*

Samuel Adams was really different: different from most people and especially different from his fellow signers of the Declaration of Independence. He was born in Boston and educated at Harvard. He had tried his hand at careers in law, commerce, and brewing. Nothing unusual in all this, unless it was his consistent lack of success. What really made Sam Adams different was his zeal. Unlike other patriot leaders, Sam never had much time for anything but the struggle for independence. The state of his bank balance proved it. While most of the other signers had devoted much of their early lives to acquiring some wealth and social status, Adams had been stirring the pot of revolution.

Adams's favorite technique was the organization of political meetings and rallies that he quickly enlarged into furious outbreaks of public resentment against some real or fancied British wrong. At this sort of thing he was a genius, and the Boston Massacre of 1770 was his masterpiece.

The casual observer would not have suspected these hidden volcanoes in Sam Adams. He was mild-mannered enough, pleasant and kindly towards others, and extremely simple in his life style. But there were those who knew him better, and they made sure that he went to the First Continental Congress in 1774, even though they had to outfit him with new clothes for the occasion. The thought of a new suit, these admirers well knew, would never occur to Sam, preoccupied as he was with his endless schemes for American freedom.

But Sam Adams, although invaluable in winning independence, had much lesser talents to bring to the task of building a new nation. Once independence was approved on July 2, 1776, he began to fade into the background. His job was really done and, except for serving briefly as governor and supporting the Federal Constitution, he never again played a prominent role on the national scene. Like Patrick Henry, another early radical, Sam Adams closed his life as a conservative. Maybe this was because, as his cousin John Adams once said, one revolution was enough for the lifetime of any man. Even for fiery Sam, the old blaze had died out by the time he breathed his last at the age of 81.

Sam Adams

JOHN ADAMS
Massachusetts

October 19, 1735   *July 4, 1826*

"He means well for his country, is always an honest man, often a wise one; but sometimes, and in some things, absolutely out of his senses." Thus shrewd Benjamin Franklin saw John Adams. Another contemporary, Richard Stockton of New Jersey, spoke of Adams as "the Atlas" of independence, the one who carried the heaviest load. The others simply helped him out.

How was Adams, irritating as he could often be, able to bear so much of this burden? Well, he was transparently honest. No one ever wondered what John Adams had up his sleeve; everything was on the table in full view. Further, he was a tireless worker with a fine clear mind. Maybe most important of all was his remarkable wife, Abigail Smith Adams, a great person in her own right.

Had it not been for Abigail and the letters her husband wrote to her, we might not have known another side of John: his sympathy, his affection, his enthusiasm. These all poured out in letter after letter as he tried to embrace this great woman across the hundreds, or even thousands, of miles that often separated them.

Honesty, intelligence, perseverance, Abigail—these props gave Adams a strength that never failed him. Despite his vanity, his pomposity, his narrowmindedness, subsequent years saw him in the roles of diplomat, Vice-President, President, and revered elder statesman. His virtues far outweighed his faults in the balance of history.

Adams in the evening of his long life is especially appealing. The fierce political battles that had brought out the worst in him were over; his broken friendship with Thomas Jefferson was restored, and the two venerable patriots loved to write to each other about the aristocracy of virtue and merit—the greatness of people for *what* they were, not *who* they were. Surely both belonged to that true nobility.

In his last letter to the doughty New Englander, Jefferson requested that his grandson, visiting Boston, might pay his respects to Adams because, "Like other young people, he wants to be able in the winter nights of old age, to recount to those around him what he had heard and learnt of the heroic age preceding his birth, and which of the Argonauts individually he was in time to have seen." An Argonaut, a heroic mariner on a perilous voyage; just the right word for John Adams, the great navigator of independence.

John Adams

ROBERT TREAT PAINE
Massachusetts

March 11, 1731   *May 11, 1814*

Being strait-laced can be embarrassing at times. Robert Treat Paine knew all about this. He was once arrested for traveling on Sunday to the site of a court where he was due the following day. If he seems merely to have been the unwitting victim of an excessively puritanical law, it must be remembered that one of the law's fervent proponents in the Massachusetts legislature had been Robert Treat Paine.

This signer was a transplanted Bostonian who moved to Taunton and there began practising law. He represented this town in the Provincial Assemblies of 1773-1775 and, after independence, in the State Legislature (1777-1778). He was a delegate to both Continental Congresses and early took his inflexible stand for American independence. When the British soldiers accused of the Boston Massacre went on trial (1770), Paine was appointed a prosecuting attorney. The equally patriotic John Adams, fearful that the Englishmen would be denied a fair trial, headed their defense. These two future signers of the Declaration of Independence, opponents in 1770, would stand side by side in 1776.

Paine, no relation to Tom Paine, author of *Common Sense,* remained a leading figure in Massachusetts public life until the end of the 18th Century. He was the state's first Attorney General (1777) and a member of the committee to draft a state constitution (1778-1780). As might be expected of one holding his conservative views, Paine was a Federalist.

It can hardly be claimed that this signer was a popular man. His blunt frankness was seldom ingratiating, and his capacity for argumentation led his Congressional colleagues to dub him "the Objection Maker." His narrowmindedness even estranged his son, Robert, Jr., a literary figure of some importance. But Paine was respected. It could not have been otherwise with one who had displayed talents in such diverse fields as law, astronomy, gunpowder production, and Indian diplomacy.

By 1804, when he retired from active politics, Paine had returned to Boston to spend his last years "in daily converse with aristocratic fellow Federalists." When the end came, the old patriot's remains were laid to rest in the famous Old Granary Burial Ground, just a few steps from the site of his birth eighty-three years before.

ELBRIDGE GERRY
Massachusetts

July 17, 1744   *November 23, 1814*

That Elbridge Gerry, a Marblehead merchant should specialize in fish seemed reasonable enough. Most Marblehead merchants did. But Gerry would in time do more than sell fish, and not everything he was to do would be quite so foreseeable. His devotion to the cause of independence, owing much to the influence of Sam Adams, that incomparable maker of rebels, would prove lasting. But the course Gerry's devotion took would have many twists and turns.

Take the night of April 18, 1775. After warning John Hancock that the British might try to interrupt his courtship of Dolly Quincy in Lexington, Gerry settled down to a secure night's sleep in Arlington. Apparently Paul Revere's ride missed him, for it was a desperately unprepared Gerry who fled at the last minute into a nearby cornfield, clad only in his nightshirt. He narrowly eluded a detachment of British troopers out to make a really good night's work of it by scooping up both him and Hancock. Happily for both the American cause and Hancock's romance, the Redcoats caught neither.

Gerry's subsequent career included extensive service in Congress, participation in the Constitutional Convention in 1787, diplomatic service abroad, and the governorship of his state. His capacity for inconsistency showed up in each case. In Congress he flitted from one side to the other on questions like maintaining a standing army and preserving the French alliance. In 1787, after working for months on it, he refused to sign the Federal Constitution. As a diplomat he persisted in negotiating with France after the XYZ Affair had sent his colleagues, John Marshall and Charles C. Pinckney, packing off in indignation. While governor of Massachusetts in 1812, he redistricted the state in such a way that his party, the Democratic-Republican, received a disproportionately large number of state senators. The salamander shape of one of the districts added the word "gerrymander" to our language.

Gerry died as Vice-President during Madison's second term. With him went whatever conclusions had been reached years before by one of the most sensible committees ever appointed by Congress, the committee to "collect and digest the late useful discoveries for making molasses and spirits from the juice of cornstalks"! Needless to say, Gerry had been its chairman.

Elbridge Gerry

STEPHEN HOPKINS
Rhode Island

March 7, 1707   *July 13, 1785*

Everyone who lived in Providence, Rhode Island, in 1776 knew Stephen Hopkins. After all he had lived there since 1742 and his family was the most famous one in town.

Stephen himself had been active in the American cause for years. He had advocated a union of the British Colonies as early as the Albany Congress of 1754, and in 1772, although Chief Justice of Rhode Island, he refused to order the arrest of the indignant citizens who had burned the grounded British revenue cutter *Gaspée* to the water's edge. Hopkins reasoned that *Gaspée* was one of the numerous oppressive measures employed by England against Americans, and that his fellow Rhode Islanders were well rid of such an instrument of tyranny. This attitude made him no friends in England, of course, but it did help get him elected to both Continental Congresses. At the Second Congress, when he signed the Declaration of Independence, he insisted that his shaky signature was not due to faintness of heart but to a palsy that troubled his old age. He need not have made any apologies, however. Everybody already knew how spunky the old gentleman was.

But Stephen Hopkins was not only courageous, he was versatile. For all his activity in government and politics, he found time to do such things as establish a newspaper (1762), write a history of Providence (1765), and view the passage of the planet Venus across the face of the sun (1769). In 1773 he freed his few slaves and a year later introduced into the Rhode Island Assembly a bill prohibiting the importation of any more slaves into the colony.

Hopkins was an exceptionally pleasant man as well. John Adams, who liked few people, liked him and spoke admiringly of his "wit, sense, knowledge, and good humor". Sometimes, however, Hopkins did exasperate his friends by his generous favors to political opponents. His allies felt that political charity should begin at home.

As it turned out, Hopkins lived to 78 and died a much revered man. If you had lived in Rhode Island in 1776, you would not only have known him, you would have liked him.

Step. Hopkins

WILLIAM ELLERY
Rhode Island

December 22, 1727   *February 15, 1820*

As the delegates approached to sign the engrossed copy of the Declaration of Independence, a round-faced, bespectacled colleague shifted to a position where he could get a good look at their faces. William Ellery was reassured by what he saw: each signer placed his name on the document with a firm hand, awed but unafraid. Ellery was resolute himself and appreciated this steadiness in others. Born in Newport, Ellery graduated from Harvard in 1747, and entered business in his native city shortly afterwards. He played an influential local role in the Revolution from its beginning, and paid a heavy price for his defiance of the King. Ellery's home was burned by the British in retaliation for the trouble he caused them. In Congress Ellery was active mainly in naval and commercial affairs. Nevertheless he did occasionally stand out in other contexts, as in seconding a 1784 resolution to abolish slavery. It was an action that did him no political good, but which he felt to be a moral duty.

We get glimpses now and then of Ellery's life in later years, though he rarely made the headlines. We know, for example, that he was especially fond of gardening, that he enjoyed reading Latin and Greek, and that he was proud of his excellent penmanship. But he took a dim view of elaborate ceremonies honoring military and naval heroes, saying the money were better spent on the victims of war.

Like his native state, Ellery had a mind of his own. Before Rhode Island had ratified the Federal Constitution, the last state to do so among the original thirteen, he accepted the post of Collector of Customs at Newport under the national government. While Rhode Island was still hesitating, Ellery had already made up his mind. This signer lived to the age of 92, leaving numerous descendants. Two of them, Richard Henry Dana and William Ellery Channing, became widely known in nineteenth century America as writers. The grandsons made good use of the freedom their grandfather had struggled so long to win for them.

ROGER SHERMAN
Connecticut

April 30, 1721   *July 23, 1793*

Roger Sherman's portrait makes him look grim, unsmiling, cold, and puritanical. Well, he certainly was a man of strict morality and plain dress, but he had a way of making people like him. His common sense especially was admired by colleagues like Thomas Jefferson, who once called him "a man who never said a foolish thing in his life."

Sherman's keen judgment cannot be traced to an aristocratic family background. His father was a Massachusetts farmer and Sherman's early career began as a shoemaker. But there was a persistence about the man that you had to respect. He customarily was the first to arrive at any session of Congress and the last to leave. As he put it, his job was "to sit up and rake ashes over the coals." In his methodical way he got things done, and by the end of the Revolution was one of the most influential members of Congress.

Roger Sherman had several enviable distinctions. He served, for example, on the committee of five that drafted the Declaration of Independence. Further, he was one of only six men to sign both the Declaration of Independence and the Federal Constitution, and he introduced the Connecticut compromise at the Constitutional Convention of 1787 (providing equal representation for each state in the Senate and representation according to population in the House).

There is a wonderful story about Sherman that greatly helps us understand him. On one occasion he was asked to dedicate a new bridge. It was a great day for the local people, and the ceremonies commenced solemnly with an impressive prayer followed by suitable music and the latest effort of the town poet. Then came Sherman's turn to speak. He rose slowly, faced the assembled group with dignity, and astonished everyone by turning and walking slowly out onto the middle of the bridge. After pausing there briefly he returned to his puzzled audience, mounted the podium, and said simply, "I think it will hold up all right." This shortest of speeches is an incomparable expression of reasoned optimism. Sherman tested the bridge and pronounced it sound. His whole life was like that; he tested things first, then said what he thought. He thought that the America he and his fellow Founding Fathers left us would prove sound. Over two hundred years indicate that he was right.

Roger Sherman

SAMUEL HUNTINGTON
Connecticut

July 3 (5?), 1731   *January 5, 1796*

Some people possess a spark that bursts into full flame as soon as the proper fuel becomes available. Samuel Huntington was this sort of man. A farmer's son, born in Windham and apprenticed to a local cooper at 16, he did not seem in 1750 to be at the start of a distinguished career in public service. No one could have foreseen his future as a statesman and national leader.

But an irresistible ambition drove Huntington on. He was just not satisfied with farming and barrelmaking; he wanted to study law. Limited as the local opportunities for legal training were, he gained admittance to his profession in 1758. In 1760 he moved to Norwich where the opportunities for his practice were greater than in Windham.

For five years the future signer devoted himself to the skillful but quiet practice of his profession. In 1765, however, his spark found its fuel in the Stamp Act. His indignation over this example of British oppression rapidly brought him to the fore as a leader of the resistance.

Huntington's star rose steadily after this. In 1764 he had been elected to the Connecticut General Assembly. From 1765 to 1775 he served as Justice of the Peace for New London County. Between 1773 and 1784 he functioned as a judge of the Connecticut Superior Court, and in 1784 as the state's Chief Justice. During much of this time he was also a member of Congress (1775-1784) and its President (1779-1781). From 1786 to his death ten years later he led his state as governor. Interestingly, the inaugural address at the start of his 1790 term dealt with the poor, inflation, and veteran's affairs, problems scarcely unfamiliar to today's leaders.

One thing must have disappointed him somewhat. After serving as President of Congress for two years, he had been forced by illness to resign in August 1781. He returned shortly after to Connecticut, just missing the pleasure of receiving official word of the surrender at Yorktown on October 19. But undoubtedly Samuel Huntington recognized that few had contributed more than he to this final confirmation of the Declaration of Independence and the great principles it embodies.

WILLIAM WILLIAMS
Connecticut

April 8, 1731   *August 2, 1811*

Lebanon, Connecticut, would be easily recognizable to William Williams today. Both his birthplace and the home of his mature years still stand. The old church is there too, built shortly before his death, and boasting the distinction of having been designed by native son John Trumbull, the world-famous artist best known for his paintings of Revolutionary War scenes. Most of all, the peaceful rural atmosphere remains.

In 1771, the future patriot married the daughter of Governor Jonathan Trumbull, the town's leading citizen. Except for brief periods, he passed the rest of his life here, where his father served as Congregationalist pastor for fifty-four years.

Williams was a Harvard graduate (1751) and served in the French and Indian War at Lake George (1755). He was a selectman for Lebanon (1760-1786), town clerk (1752-1796), a member of the lower house of the Connecticut legislature (1757-1776; 1781-1784), and a delegate to Congress (1776-1778; 1783-1784). Such positions, usually filled by men of local reputation, did not project Williams prominently onto the national scene, but he seems to have had no large-scale ambitions anyway. He did not make himself conspicuous in Congress, and his aspirations were apparently satisfied by the unobtrusive but effective service he rendered in the smaller arenas of community and state.

Williams was especially noted during the Revolution for his zealous efforts to provide for the American troops. Like many another patriot, he repeatedly made contributions to their welfare that entailed major personal and financial sacrifices.

One of William's early biographers tells of a conversation between the signer and one Benjamin Huntington. The latter is reported to have said that, since he had neither signed the Declaration of Independence nor written anything in opposition to the British government, he was "at all events secure from the gallows." Williams retorted fiercely, "Then, sir, you ought to be hanged for not doing your duty."

The lengthy inscription on William's tombstone gives us some indication of how his neighbors felt about him. "Eminent for his virtues and piety," "a firm, steady, and ardent friend of his country in the darkest time," "a long, honorable, and well-spent life"; this was how he looked to those who knew him best.

OLIVER WOLCOTT
Connecticut

December 1, 1726   *December 1, 1797*

In at least one way the American Revolution was unique. Its leaders, for the most part, were men who had been influential before the war began, and who retained their places of power during and after the fighting. For example, Governor Jonathan Trumbull of Connecticut, the last governor under the Crown, retained his office even after independence had been declared.

Oliver Wolcott was born in Windsor, the son of Roger Wolcott, colonial governor from 1751 to 1754. Young Wolcott studied medicine after his graduation from Yale in 1747, but instead of practicing, he accepted the post of Sheriff of Litchfield in 1751. He lived the rest of his life in this beautiful village, which elected him repeatedly to the Connecticut legislature and to the Congress.

This patriot's Revolutionary career included more military than political service. He was, for instance, in command of 14 militia regiments at Saratoga. But his political involvement was great, keeping him in Congress from 1775 to 1783, except when on military duty.

Illness forced Wolcott to take a brief leave from Congress in July 1776, just as the debates on independence reached their climax. But he did not miss out on all the excitement. On his way through New York to Litchfield, he somehow succeeded in obtaining the leaden statue of George III, pulled down by enthusiastic New Yorkers at Bowling Green, and carting it all the way to his western Connecticut home. There the ladies melted down the royal effigy and recast it as bullets to fire back at their former sovereign's troops.

After the war Wolcott remained a prominent public figure. In 1784 he signed the Treaty of Fort Stanwix (N.Y.) with the Iroquois, and in 1788 became a potent advocate of the newly proposed Federal Constitution. In 1796 he succeeded his fellow Connecticut signer, Samuel Huntington, as governor of the state.

Wolcott died in office in 1797, completing a life of public service before, during, and after the Revolution. His son, Oliver, Jr., also became a power in public life when he succeeded Alexander Hamilton as Secretary of the Treasury in 1795. Whether America was presided over by George III or by George Washington a Wolcott helped direct the course of its history.

WILLIAM FLOYD
New York

December 17, 1734   *August 4, 1821*

Brookhaven, Long Island, is famous today as the site of a laboratory known for its outstanding atomic research. In William Floyd's time it was simply a farm community with a small harbor. When his father died, the 18-year old future signer inherited one of the best pieces of property in the area. He seemed to have everything required for a secure and placid future.

But the Revolution broke out and Floyd was caught up in the struggle from the very beginning. Actually, he was not so much caught up in it as he was an active promoter of it, serving in both

Continental Congresses and playing a vigorous, if unsuccessful, military role on Long Island.

With the British occupation of Brookhaven in 1776, Floyd's family fled to Connecticut where they experienced considerable hardship. Indeed, in later years Floyd expressed the view that his wife and children might have been better off if they had stayed in Brookhaven and taken their chances with the British.

This solid, if inconspicuous, signer has one distinction that is of at least minor interest. His daughter Kitty turned down an offer of marriage from James Madison. She later wed a minister and Madison got over his disappointment by taking Dolley Payne Todd, a lively widow, as his wife.

If Kitty had a mind of her own it is easy to see where she got it. Her father, forced off his possessions in 1776, did not return to live on Long Island until 1783. A year later he purchased land in upstate New York near present-day Utica. Amazingly, in 1803, at the age of 69, Floyd uprooted himself and his family and moved onto his upstate lands. Such a step took courage, but this old patriot had shown that quality before.

Floyd died in Westernville in his 87th year. Typical of many Revolutionary leaders, his career had been unspectacular yet fervently dedicated to an America that would endure as a model for free people everywhere.

PHILIP LIVINGSTON
New York

January 15, 1716   *June 12, 1778*

From his country home on Brooklyn Heights Philip Livingston could watch his ships entering and leaving New York Harbor almost every day. He was a commercial giant, a great man, and he knew it. One look at his solemn, portly figure and others knew it too.

But Livingston combined a keen sense of public responsibility with his air of superiority. Immensely wealthy, he was also exceptionally generous. Some of his contributions to improving the life of New York were his support of King's College (later

Columbia University), and his role in the founding of the New York Society Library, the New York Hospital, and the Chamber of Commerce.

This distinguished philanthropist was equally aware of his responsibilities to the cause of America's liberty. Active in politics as early as 1754, in 1764 he joined the Assembly in petitioning for the right of New Yorkers to be taxed only with their own consent. He vigorously fought the Stamp Act in 1765, and in 1774 was elected to Congress where he served on the Treasury, Marine, Commerce, and Indian Affairs committees. It could not be said that Philip Livingston kept either his abilities or his wealth to himself; both were put at the service of his country.

Yet Livingston, generous as he really was, never inspired affection in the hearts of his fellow citizens. They respected and admired him, but from a distance. There was an air of the aristocrat about him that discouraged familiarity. Furthermore, he was neither a rabble rouser nor a crowd pleaser. The activities of the New York Sons of Liberty, often resulting in riots, disgusted him every bit as much as British violations of American rights. He valued peace as well as freedom, and constantly sought to obtain both.

Philip Livingston, not to be confused with his cousin, Robert R. Livingston, took no part in the Congressional debates on independence, but he signed the Declaration and gave himself fully to its implementation. When American military reverses in Pennsylvania in 1778 forced Congress to move briefly to York, some of the members went home. The accommodations in the little town were not quite to their liking. Livingston, the most aristocratic Congressman of all, stayed on despite grave illness. He never left York, dying there in 1778, a courageous man who knew how much he had to lose, but who willingly risked everything for the sake of his countrymen.

FRANCIS LEWIS
New York

March 21, 1713   *December 31, 1802*

It did not take much to bring out the rebel in Francis Lewis. Born in Wales, he had from early childhood absorbed the Welshman's distrust of England and was always keenly sensitive to the least hint of British oppression.

Nonetheless, Lewis's early life gave little indication of his future course. He came to New York in the 1730's and, after a difficult start, became so prosperous a merchant by 1765 that he was able to retire to his country home at Whitestone, Long Island. His retirement coincided with the proclamation of the

Stamp Act, and Lewis, now possessed of a little leisure, became heated by the flames of resentment to the point of joining the radical Sons of Liberty. The respectable businessman was quickly transformed into a vigorous revolutionary.

The Revolution, when it came, bit deeply into Lewis's personal life. While he was attending Congress in 1776 his Whitestone home was ransacked by British troops and his wife taken captive. Mrs. Lewis was badly treated, even being denied such simple necessities as clean clothes for weeks at a time. The health of the elderly woman was so undermined by her ordeal that she died in 1779.

Another of Lewis's trials, the problem of divided family loyalties, was common to many American patriots. Much to her father's distress, one of Lewis's daughters married a Captain Robinson of the Royal Navy and lived the rest of her life in England. A father's affection, however, seems to have overcome his resentment at what he must have considered his daughter's disloyalty, for each year Mrs. Robinson received a generous gift from an anonymous donor in New York. No one doubted the identity of her benefactor.

Francis Lewis shared a maddening frustration with the other three New York signers. They were unable to participate in the debates on independence or to vote for it: their instructions from the New York legislature forbade it. Fortunately, the prohibition was withdrawn in mid-July, and Lewis and his colleagues signed on August 2, 1776.

This signer passed his last years quietly. Although his wealth was much depleted by the war, his health remained good almost to the day of his death, age 89, in New York City.

LEWIS MORRIS
New York

April 8, 1726   *January 22, 1798*

There would seem to have been little reason for Lewis Morris to embrace the Revolutionary cause. His grandfather had been the first Royal Governor of New Jersey. His father was a wealthy, influential member of New York's political and social aristocracy. His brother was a British army officer. But Lewis Morris, born to the purple as he was, embraced the American cause early in the struggle.

It may have been that Morris did not particularly like his fellow aristocrats, the Philipses and the Delanceys. Since they were Tories he might have felt drawn toward the rebel side. Yet Morris's involvement in the Revolution was too deep to have been the result of mere perversity. In 1775 he led a delegation from Westchester to the New York Provincial assembly. In the same year he was sent to Congress, and later travelled from Philadelphia to deal with several potentially hostile Indian tribes. In 1776 he was appointed a Brigadier General of New York militia.

When the Declaration of Independence was voted on, Morris was at the New York Provincial assembly in White Plains. This assembly was important because, on July 9, 1776, it rescinded the instructions to New York's Congressional delegates which had forbidden them to vote for independence. As soon as Morris got back to Philadelphia after this, probably in September, he added his name to the Declaration's list of signatures.

The atmosphere in Lewis Morris's home must have been highly favorable to independence. His son, also Lewis, served with distinction as an aide to General John Sullivan in his expedition against the Iroquois (1779), and under General Nathanael Greene during his brilliant Southern campaign (1781).

This signer spent his last years managing business affairs from Morrisania, his home in what is now The Bronx, New York, and wondering what to expect next from his brilliant but unconventional half-brother Gouverneur. The latter, a framer of the Federal Constitution, was cast in a different mold, but their separate paths ran together in 1788 when Lewis vigorously assisted Alexander Hamilton in winning New York ratification of the country's new Constitution.

The two Morrises, Lewis and Gouverneur, twenty-six years apart by birth and eighteen by death, now lie near each other at St. Ann's Episcopal Church in The Bronx.

Lewis Morris

RICHARD STOCKTON
New Jersey

October 1, 1730   *February 28, 1781*

Richard Stockton dearly loved his prize horses. He loved his art collection and his library too, but the horses were especially close to his heart. In fact, his opponents charged that he valued these superb animals even more than he did his country. This, according to the rumor, explained why he narrowly missed being elected first American governor of New Jersey. Word had got around that he refused to turn several of his finest specimens over to the service of the American army.

Well, if the story is true, it contrasts strongly with subsequent events in Stockton's life. He was elected to Congress in June 1776 and served on a committee to inspect the Northern Army in the fall of that same year. On his return to New Jersey, he found the British in possession of his home area near Princeton. He managed to get his family away to safety, but was himself betrayed and captured at the home of a friend in Monmouth.

The capture of a Declaration signer brought out the worst in Stockton's British captors. They took him first to Perth Amboy and later to New York where he felt the full force of their vengeance. The brutality of his treatment came to the attention of Congress, which protested formally to Sir William Howe. General Washington was instructed to secure Stockton's exchange as a prisoner of war. Unfortunately, his harrowing experience had totally broken his health, and he lived out his last few years as an invalid.

America lost an experienced public servant with Stockton's imprisonment and death. He had previously been a member of the Provincial Congress of New Jersey and a justice of that colony's Supreme Court. He was also a gifted lawyer, greatly in demand, and a loyal alumnus of the college of New Jersey (now Princeton), which he supported most generously. In fact, he had been influential in getting Dr. John Witherspoon, another signer of the Declaration, to come to America˙and assume the presidency of Princeton in 1768.

Richard Stockton was called on to endure intense suffering for his loyalty to the American cause. If he had been reluctant to put a few horses at the service of his country, he certainly did not spare himself.

JOHN WITHERSPOON
New Jersey

February 5, 1723   *November 15, 1794*

John Witherspoon very nearly did not get a chance to sign the Declaration of Independence. In fact, if Mrs. Witherspoon had had her way, he would never have left his native Scotland. As it was, two future signers of the Declaration, Richard Stockton and Benjamin Rush, just barely succeeded in persuading this distinguished Presbyterian minister to come to America and assume the presidency of the College of New Jersey (now Princeton University). From 1768 to 1794, whatever else he did, he conscientiously devoted himself to developing and improving that renowned institution.

Dr. Witherspoon almost did not get to sign the Declaration for another reason. He was not elected to Congress until June 22, 1776, well after the resolutions advocating independence had been introduced. But the minute he delivered his first speech everybody knew how he felt about the great question. Taking issue with more cautious Congressmen, he stated emphatically that America was "not only ripe for independence but rotting for the want of it."

John Witherspoon, the only clergyman of any denomination in the Continental Congress, was a man of definite opinions. He believed, for example, that education should fit a person for a life of service to others. He also favored thrift in government, common sense in religion, and the Federal Constitution of 1787. Perhaps nothing better illustrates his individuality than his insistence on wearing clerical garb at Congressional sessions. He knew who he was and what he represented, and he never hesitated to let others know where he stood.

One quality of this underrated Founding Father was of enormous value during the trying early years of independence. A kindly reconciler of quarrels, he frequently succeeded in restoring sorely needed harmony. He had his share of sorrow too, losing a son at the Battle of Germantown (1777) and going blind during the last two years of his life. But this sturdy patriot took the good with the bad, never losing confidence in the validity of his principles or the ultimate triumph of American liberty.

FRANCIS HOPKINSON
New Jersey

October 2, 1737   *May 9, 1791*

Francis Hopkinson, one of the most versatile 18th century Americans, was born in Philadelphia. His father is said to have demonstrated the "electrical fluid" in lightning even before Benjamin Franklin's famous experiment with the kite and key. This family interest in science was passed on to Francis, who busied himself endlessly with activities like manufacturing artificial pearls, raising pigeons, and observing the workings of the earliest Delaware River steamboat. From this, one might expect that Hopkinson was a professional naturalist, but such was not the case at all. This New Jersey signer was actually a lawyer by profession, and a very good one. His success in that career led to his being elected to the Continental Congress in 1776, just in time to vote for independence and sign the Declaration. Although born in Philadelphia and a frequenter of that city, Hopkinson in 1776 was living in Bordentown, New Jersey. Hence his election to Congress from that state. Can we adequately describe Francis Hopkinson by saying that he was a moderately important political leader with natural science as his hobby? Not quite, because this would overlook the fact that he was so accomplished a musician that he gave public recitals on the harpsichord and served for several years as principal organist at Christ Church in Philadelphia. In fact, he even composed a few pieces, and one of his songs, "My Days Have Been So Wondrous Free," can still be found in some books of old American songs.

But there is more yet. Hopkinson was a poet, probably the first American novelist, and an artist of more than a little talent. You could hardly ask anybody to be much more versatile than that. The only other signers with a similarly broad range of interests and abilities were Franklin and Jefferson. No one would claim that Hopkinson was as great as either of these giants, yet he was a friend of both and corresponded regularly with them. Some of his witty letters to Jefferson in Paris make delightful reading even today. Hopkinson's last years were passed in Philadelphia, living with a daughter. He died there of a stroke at the age of 53. America lost a delightful and gifted patriot when he was laid to rest in Christ Church cemetery in Philadelphia in 1791.

JOHN HART
New Jersey

? 1711   *May 11, 1779*

There is much we do not know about John Hart, though it now seems certain he was born in Stonington, Connecticut. Further, although his biographers depict him as a bluff, rugged farmer, his portrait shows him as delicate, almost effeminate. It is unfortunate that we cannot see the plain, weatherbeaten man of 65 who signed the Declaration of Independence.

The son of a father once outstandingly devoted to the King, this signer entered the struggle for independence in 1765. In that year, reaction to the Stamp Act was prompt and forceful. Hart, a member of New Jersey's legislature, asserted bluntly that laws imposed by Parliament on unrepresented people were in no way binding on free men.

In 1774 this farmer and mill owner from western New Jersey was elected to both the First Provincial Congress and the First Continental Congress. The following year he was sent to the Second Continental Congress, and in 1776 promoted the expulsion of Royal Governor William Franklin (Benjamin's son). When New Jersey formed its First State Assembly after independence, John Hart was chosen Speaker.

In December 1776, after capturing New York, the British swept through New Jersey. Hart rushed to his home in Hopewell only to find his wife dying. Friends had to tear him from her bedside and hide him in the nearby hills to prevent his capture. Once there, however, there was nowhere else to go, and he wandered for weeks from cave to barn to farmhouse, never staying long enough in one place to be seen and betrayed. For a man of 65 a British jail would almost surely have proved fatal, yet Hart needed remarkable toughness to survive what he did. Perhaps the best indication of this sturdiness was his success in preserving a sense of humor. Once, forced to stay in a barn overnight, he found himself in the company of a large friendly dog. Hart later described him as a companion "not in those evil times the most exceptionable." At least the animal was no Tory sympathizer.

This notably religious man was one of the first signers to die. Before his death he presented the Hopewell Baptist congregation with land for a church and graveyard. They are both still there, durable as the heritage of freedom John Hart left to all of us.

John Hart

ABRAHAM CLARK
New Jersey

February 15, 1726   *September 15, 1794*

Abraham Clark, a man of strong convictions, knew what it meant to make sacrifices. He had little education, but he did have principles. For instance, he regarded honesty, thrift, and independence as cardinal public virtues. He held equally firmly to another principle that would cause him much anguish. Clark did not believe that men in public office should use their positions to confer favors on members of their personal families. Being a son or daughter of Abraham Clark entitled you to his affection, but not his patronage. Independent himself, he expected other adults to be so too. During the course of the

Revolution two of his sons, both army officers, were captured by the British. It need hardly be said that the commissions held by the younger Clarks had not been gained through any paternal influence. But the knowledge that they were in British hands was agonizing to their father who was well aware of the grim reputation of British jails and prison ships. It is said that the British offered the release of the two sons in exchange for their father's defection to the Tory side. The unhappy man, not even tempted by such crude bait, must have keenly felt the frustration of his helplessness. But he stuck to his principle of no special privilege. Clark even refused to request the government to intercede specifically in his case. Eventually Congress did obtain the exchange of the two prisoners, but only on the insistence of others.

Abraham Clark's career was not complex. Born the only son of a farmer, he was thrown on his own early in life. He worked for a time as a surveyor and later studied law. It is not certain whether he was ever formally admitted to legal practice, but he was enough of a lawyer to gain a reputation as "the poor man's counselor." Whether his legal business was formal or unofficial, it earned him so solid a local reputation that he was elected to the New Jersey Committee of Safety, the Provincial Congress, and the Continental Congress. He was even elected to the Constitutional Convention of 1787, but illness prevented his attendence. Clearly Clark commanded the confidence of those who knew him. This signer died from sunstroke suffered while watching the construction of a bridge near his home in Elizabeth.

ROBERT MORRIS
Pennsylvania

January 31, 1734   *May 8, 1806*

Robert Morris was not easily convinced. But once he reached a decision he stuck with it. In 1776, when separation from England was being debated, he opposed the whole idea. Yet he changed his mind and signed the Declaration a month after independence was voted. From then on, few equaled his contribution toward assuring that the United States would one day be more than a fond hope.

Morris was a financial wizard. His phenomenal business success for more than twenty years before the Revolution left no doubt about that. In 1781, therefore, he was appointed Superintendent of Finance by Congress, a post he held until 1784. He resigned then, frustrated by his inability to persuade the individual states to meet their financial obligations to the national government. Genius had been required in Morris's position by the simple fact that here were no finances to supervise. As was the case during the Yorktown campaign of 1781, he frequently had to use his own money or credit to keep the country going. One observer marveled at Morris's skill in "dazzling the public eye by the same piece of coin, multiplied by a thousand reflectors."

In 1787 Morris enjoyed the privilege of signing the Federal Constitution as a delegate from Pennsylvania. He thus became one of only six men to sign both the Declaration and the Constitution.

For all his ability, however, Morris ultimately came to financial grief by overspeculating in western lands. Hoping to resell them at a handsome profit, Morris, like many others, bought vast tracts of territory in the expectation that they would rapidly be settled. They were not. In an effort to save his investments, he overextended his resources, spending money he did not have, and plunging ever deeper into debt. His vast fortune soon vanished, a casualty of his failure to use the keen business judgment he had previously shown.

By 1798 Morris, at the mercy of his creditors, was carried off to debtors' prison. There he remained for over three years, defeated and humiliated, an utterly broken man. Even after his release he never held his head up again. It was a sad ending to the career of a great patriot. The man who had so often saved the country by his generosity was in turn left unaided in his own hour of greatest need.

BENJAMIN RUSH
Pennsylvania

January 4, 1746   *April 19, 1813*

Many people did not like Benjamin Rush. One was Dr. William Shippen, Director-General of Medicine in the Continental Army, whom Rush accused of mismanagement. That was the way with Rush; he came out and told you what he thought, whether you liked it or not.

But there is much to be said in favor of this signer. He was probably the best trained and best known American physician of his day. He earned his M.D. from the famous medical school in Edinburgh, Scotland, at a time when most of his colleagues had no formal medical training at all, and he subsequently taught at both the College of Philadelphia and the University of Pennsylvania.

In January 1776 Rush married a daughter of New Jersey signer Richard Stockton. In June he was named to the Pennsylvania Provincial Congress, and one month later to the Continental Congress, too late to vote for independence, but in time to sign the Declaration.

Rush possessed great humanitarian instincts. He was president of the Pennsylvania Society for Promoting the Abolition of Slavery, advocated improved education for women, and labored long hours to make life better for the mentally ill. One of these unfortunates, his son John, was a naval officer who lost his reason after killing a fellow officer in a duel.

Benjamin Rush was also a man of courage. Late in the 18th century Philadelphia was struck by several dreadful epidemics of yellow fever. The worst was in 1793. Many people, including physicians, who could leave town did so. Not Rush. Although he really had no cure for the disease, he stayed on and did his best.

At the end of his life Rush achieved one more great thing, the reconciliation of Thomas Jefferson and John Adams, estranged by years of political warfare. Rush venerated both these great men and grieved to see their former friendship in ruins. With a little tact and diplomacy he got the two of them to write to each other. The former affection quickly revived and the two old patriots appreciated Rush's intervention. Jefferson put their feelings well when he informed Adams of their mutual friend's death:

> "Another of our friends of seventy-six is gone ... another of the co-signers of the Independence of our country. ... A better man than Rush could not have left us, more benevolent, more learned, ... or more honest."

BENJAMIN FRANKLIN
Pennsylvania

January 17, 1706   *April 17, 1790*

Like most people, Benjamin Franklin was sometimes wise and sometimes foolish, sometimes noble and sometimes petty. But unlike most of us, he was authentically great: great in ability, great in understanding, and great in the service he rendered his country.

Franklin, the oldest signer of the Declaration, was more than six months beyond his seventieth birthday when he put his signature to the document. One would have had to predict then that this would prove the climactic ending of a career in which he had already attained greatness as a publisher, scientist, philosopher, and statesman. There just seemed no way for a man of his age to go on to greater things. But Franklin confounded everyone by reaching new heights twice again, both times in the selfless service of his country.

Franklin's first great achievement after the Declaration came as Minister to France (1776-1785). During this critical decade he secured French recognition of American independence and her indispensable assistance in the war against England. General Washington, great as he was, probably could not have won the struggle without this help.

The other triumph of this tireless elder statesman occurred at the Constitutional Convention of 1787. There he repeatedly soothed ruffled tempers, reconciled differences, and suggested compromises. His imperturbable good humor, despite intense physical pain, repeatedly kept short tempers and summer heat from ruining the chance to build a strong durable nation.

What made Franklin great above even his greatest contemporaries? Probably his sympathetic understanding of human nature. He was neither vain like John Adams nor touchy like Jefferson. Rather, his amiable manner drew both the gifted and the dull into displaying talents they never before knew they had. Even in holding off busybodies who should have known better he showed a tactful good humor that left no injured feelings. In reply to a clergyman who quizzed Franklin on his religious views the old patriot could well have stated that such were no one's business but his own. Instead, he good-naturedly answered that he did not propose to engage in theological speculation in his old age, for a brief wait would undoubtedly put him in possession of the answers. Franklin, beloved in his time and ours, has been woven by history into the very fabric of America.

JOHN MORTON
Pennsylvania

c. 1724   *April ?, 1777*

The vote of Pennsylvania on independence was as important as it was uncertain. It was important because Pennsylvania was the largest of the commercial Middle States and because, since the vote would be taken in geographical order of states from north to south, Pennsylvania's vote, added to that of her more northern neighbors, could produce the majority for independence. However, the Pennsylvania delegation was a puzzle. Franklin and Wilson were for independence, but Dickinson, Morris, Willing, and Humphrey were, with varying degrees of firmness, against it. John Morton was the big question mark. As it developed, on the day the voting began (July 2, 1776), Dickinson and Morris stayed home. There it was: two for, two against, and Morton.

Thus it was up to an honest, conscientious delegate of Swedish ancestry to make the decision one way or the other. John Morton was no novice in public affairs. He had held office in his native Chester County, served in the Provincial Assembly and both Continental Congresses, and sat as an Associate Justice on the Pennsylvania Supreme Court. But he had never been in a situation quite like this. As it turned out, he voted in the affirmative, the Pennsylvania delegation thereafter supported independence, and the die of our national existence was cast. Morton at the critical moment pointed out the road to liberty.

But while John Morton, a conservative "law and order" man, eventually embraced independence wholeheartedly, not all his friends did. Fearful of their economic and social interests, they censured their former friend for his vote. Morton replied, according to the inscription on his tombstone, "Tell them that they will live to see the hour when they shall acknowledge it to have been the most glorious service that I have rendered to my country."

While his skeptical friends may have lived long enough to enjoy American independence, Morton did not. Of the nine signers of the Declaration to die before the victory at Yorktown, Morton went first, dying in April 1777. This one-time farmer never expected that breaking the ground for independence would be easy. But having put his hand to the plow, he did not turn back.

John Morton

GEORGE CLYMER
Pennsylvania

March 16, 1739   *January 24, 1813*

Charles Willson Peale, a patriot himself, liked to paint portraits of other patriots. The one he did of George Clymer shows a calm, self-possessed man of determination. There is a quiet look about the eyes and a firmness of the jaw that bespeak one who accomplishes much while making little noise.

Although Clymer had no ambition at all for public office, his reputation as a leading Philadelphia merchant thrust him forward nonetheless. Despite having been orphaned before his first birthday, he made his way up the ladder from countinghouse clerk to partnership in Reese Meredith & Son, one of Philadelphia's great business establishments. Further, Clymer married Elizabeth Meredith in 1765, thus linking himself to his partner by marital as well as financial ties.

George Clymer, who served on the Pennsylvania Council of Safety (1775-1776), went to Congress as one of five replacements for the Pennsylvania delegates who had opposed independence. The arrival of the new group after the vote had been taken indicated at how late an hour the Pennsylvania legislature had changed its mind.

One widely recognized talent of this signer was his ability to carry out assignments demanding extreme tact. Thus he was chosen to look into the problems of the disease-plagued, dissension-ridden Northern Army in 1776. In 1777-1778 he undertook to investigate the growing disaffection in western Pennsylvania that threatened to throw that whole area open to marauding bands of Tory-led Indians. A later mission of similar delicacy attempted to uncover the leaders of the Whisky Rebellion in 1794.

One of Clymer's historic distinctions is that he was one of four Pennsylvanians to sign both the Declaration of Independence and the Federal Constitution. On the humanitarian side, his work in moderating Pennsylvania's penal code was outstanding. So were his roles as a founder of the Philadelphia Academy of the Fine Arts and the Philadelphia Agricultural Society.

George Clymer served in the first House of Representatives under the new Constitution. Yet he was never anybody's man but his own, and viewed his role as one in whict to think *for* the people, not merely *with* them. Clymer was one of our most effective if least remembered Founding Fathers.

JAMES SMITH
Pennsylvania

1719 ?   *July 11, 1806*

When Pennsylvanians grew restless at the opposition to independence of some of their Congressional delegates, a housecleaning seemed in order. Thus, in July 1776, after the break with England had been finally decided upon, new delegates were elected. One of them was James Smith, a frontier lawyer from York, who had also engaged in the iron smelting business.

Smith was amiable but eccentric, steadfastly refusing ever to tell anyone his age. Seventeen nineteen is merely a reasonable guess at the year of his birth. Yet his ability to regale tavern, courtroom, and legislative hall with tale after tale kept him in constant demand. Eccentric or not, he was excellent for morale wherever he went.

It should not be thought, however, that Smith's sole contribution to American independence was entertainment. Born in Northern Ireland, he came to America as a boy with his father. The youthful immigrant attended school in Philadelphia and was admitted to law practice there in 1745. Around 1750 he moved to York where he continued his legal practice and speculated in the ironworks. His public services included participation in Provincial conventions in 1775 and 1776, and raising a York militia company. A supporter of the ultra-democratic Pennsylvania Constitution of 1776, Smith served in the Pennsylvania State Assembly (1779) and as a judge of the state's High Court of Errors and Appeals (1780-1781).

If Smith's name is not written in large bold letters on the pages of history, it may be in part because his reputation was made in the frontier town of York rather than in influential Philadelphia. Perhaps, too, it is because Smith's home and papers were destroyed by fire in 1805, the year before his death. In any case, his role in the Revolution was honorable and useful, and his sprightly personality frequently relieved tensions and averted crises. It took all kinds to make independence a reality, including those who, like James Smith, played indispensable lesser roles in the great drama.

GEORGE TAYLOR
Pennsylvania

1716   *February 23, 1781*

So little is known about George Taylor's early life that we can specify neither the exact date nor the precise place of his birth. He seems to have come from Northern Ireland; arriving in Philadelphia about 1736 as an indentured servant. He worked off his bond, first as a laborer and later as a clerk, at an ironworks in Chester County. He did remarkably well in this early industrial enterprise, and after its owner died, married the widow and took over the business. Later he also engaged in iron manufacturing in nearby Bucks County.

Taylor's political roles were always minor but seldom insignificant. Of interest is the fact that he was regarded as having some expertise in matters relating to the Indians. Perhaps this was because early in life Taylor had been a leader in obtaining the punishment of some renegade whites guilty of murdering several Indians. His prominence in bringing these criminals to justice earned him a reputation for fairness and impartiality in his dealings with the local tribes. He was thus a logical choice for the Congressional committee appointed to treat with the Indians at Easton, Pennsylvania, in 1777.

The reputation today of many of the Declaration signers rests on their lasting achievements while often there is little in the way of material evidence that they ever lived. For instance, no original home of Benjamin Franklin's exists now, but his fame endures undiminished. With George Taylor the opposite situation holds. His career in Congress was brief and his impact on the early history of his country slight. But three Pennsylvania homes of Taylor's still survive. One is in Catasaqua on the Lehigh River. The others are in Easton and Durham. Each home is solid and durable. The ones in Catasaqua and Durham are moderately large; the one in Easton is small. Perhaps this is symbolic of the sturdiness of both large and small states in the independent America which George Taylor helped form.

Even more important than the symbolism of Taylor's homes is the implication of his life. His road from penniless immigrant to respected leader was certainly an unusual and an admirable progression. And this same road, seldom an easy one, has been followed by countless newcomers to our shores ever since Taylor's day.

JAMES WILSON
Pennsylvania

September 14, 1742   *August 21, 1798*

One of the unfortunate developments of American history is the obscurity into which James Wilson has fallen. He was, it is true, changeable and cranky, but nonetheless he ranks as one of the greatest of the Founding Fathers.

Wilson, who was born and educated in Scotland, came to America in 1765. He studied law in Philadelphia under John Dickinson and proved an extraordinary pupil. In his first court case Wilson defeated Benjamin Chew, a leader of the Pennsylvania bar. The signer later moved his practice to Carlisle where his great talents put him at the undisputed head of his profession.

But James Wilson was not unaware of the approaching storm of the Revolution. He long pondered the question of independence and, in 1774, published a pamphlet on the extent to which Parliament could legislate for the colonies. This booklet, strongly advocating separation from England, was distributed to Wilson's fellow delegates at the First Continental Congress.

Then doubts crept in. By the time Richard Henry Lee presented his independence resolutions in June 1776, Wilson had changed his mind. He now opposed independence. When it came up for the vote, however, he reversed himself one last time, supporting the Lee Resolutions, and leaving it up to John Morton to cast Pennsylvania's deciding vote.

Much turbulence marked Wilson's later career. Though he continued to endorse independence, he lost faith in popular government, especially as embodied in the Pennsylvania Constitution of 1776. Here his testiness made numerous enemies and led to the 1779 "Affair of Fort Wilson" when a pro-Constitution mob laid siege to his house. It took a troop of mounted militia to rescue him.

The climax of Wilson's career came at the Constitutional Convention of 1787. His contribution to developing the Federal charter was equaled only by that of James Madison. Subsequently, Wilson drove the constitution through the Pennsylvania ratifying convention on December 12, 1787, chagrined that Delaware had beaten him to it by ratifying six days earlier.

Unhappily, the clouds never quite lifted for Wilson. Early speculations in western lands eventually caught up with him and although he served with distinction on the first Supreme Court, his last years were bedeviled by relentless creditors. He died in Edenton, North Carolina, harried and distraught, attended to by his sympathetic colleague, Justice James Iredell.

James Wilson

GEORGE ROSS
Pennsylvania

May 10, 1730   *July 14, 1779*

Although George Ross was born in New Castle, Delaware, history associates him with western Pennsylvania. Not western as we would use the term today, however; Ross lived in Lancaster, only about 60 miles from Philadelphia. It is hard to believe that America's 1776 frontier was that close to her largest city.

Ross studied law in Philadelphia and began his practice in Lancaster in 1750, at the age of 20. He married the following year and entered the Provincial Assembly in 1768. Like George Taylor of Easton, another signer from the Pennsylvania "frontier," Ross was much interested in Indian affairs. He also strongly opposed a series of arbitrary actions by the Governor, and advocated appealing to the King to change Pennsylvania's government from Proprietary to Crown. This position gained Ross a reputation as a Tory. In fact, when he was sent to the First Continental Congress in 1774, he was regarded as an opponent of independence.

But Ross was no such thing. His turning toward the King was motivated solely by what the Lancaster lawyer regarded as the Governor's illegal actions. When it became evident that the King himself was perfectly capable of oppression, Ross shifted his position decisively. In 1775 he was named to the Pennsylvania Committee of Safety and in 1776 elected to the Second Continental Congress, a more independence-minded assembly than its predecessor.

Ross was plagued with ill health, however, and according to Benjamin Rush at least, a lack of that dogged patience needed by any effective legislator. He must have been an honest public officer all the same. When he retired from Congress in 1777 the citizens of Lancaster County attempted to present him with a generous financial reward for his services. He declined, saying that he had done only his duty and was entitled to no recompense beyond his regular salary.

This signer died in Philadelphia after suffering from gout for many years. This fact, combined with contemporary accounts of his genial temperament and convivial nature, lead one to surmise that George Ross was a man who delighted in good living. Although exceptionally popular in his own time, he has now almost faded from our national memory.

CAESAR RODNEY
Delaware

October 7, 1728   *June 26, 1784*

You could hardly imagine a more dramatic situation! By the evening of July 1, 1776, Congress had come to a final vote on the resolutions declaring America independent. The next day would determine whether the colonies still retained their uncomfortable allegiance to Great Britain or whether a new nation would be born. The question was especially difficult for little Delaware.

The three Lower Counties, as Delaware was often called then, had sent three delegates to Congress. One of them, Caesar Rodney, was not in Philadelphia on this fateful July 1, however, but back home putting down a local Tory uprising. Rodney was a soldier as well as a statesman, and this was one time when his military duties unavoidably kept him away from Congress. Thomas McKean, however, was in Congress, and he was worried. Although he and Rodney favored independence, the third Delaware delegate, George Read, did not. Without Rodney, the opposing votes of McKean and Read balanced each other and left Delaware without an effective voice on the question. McKean was not the sort of man to stand for that. Therefore, at his own expense, he hired a horseman to ride the 80 miles from Philadelphia to Rodney's home near Dover that very night.

McKean's message came late, but Rodney needed no instructions in what to do. Saddling up immediately, he rode for hours, urging his horses, one after another, to their maximum efforts.

When the voting began on the next afternoon, Rodney had still not arrived. McKean knew he would come, but would he be in time? He was; just barely, for Rodney rushed into the hall to vote without even waiting to remove his boots and spurs.

This was the most dramatic thing that ever happened to Caesar Rodney. But there is one more thing we should remember about him. He spent the last decade of his life tragically afflicted with cancer. Siding with the cause of independence ruled out all possibility of his being treated by the best English doctors. Rodney gladly accepted this as a personal sacrifice for his country.

Delaware has honored this leader by placing his statue in the National Capitol in Washington, a fitting tribute to a courageous, likable man who loved young people, hated slavery, told wonderful stories, and did his heroic best for American freedom.

GEORGE READ
Delaware

September 18, 1733   *September 21, 1798*

George Read could be terribly stubborn at times. For example, he held out to the very end in opposing American independence. This tenacity impelled Thomas McKean to summon Caesar Rodney to break the Delaware deadlock on the great question. Rodney's reply was his famous ride from Dover to Philadelphia. But George Read was no "sunshine patriot." Once the issue of independence had been resolved, he supported America's cause wholeheartedly. Not only did he sign the Declaration, but eleven years later he participated significantly in the Constitutional Convention. His main contribution to the structure of the Federal government was his support of equal representation for all states, large and small, in the new Senate. However, he stirred up a real storm at one stage of the Convention by proposing the abolishment of state boundaries in order to unite the new country. He was far out of step with the views of his colleagues in that sally.

It is probable that George Read would have made a fine actor. Not only did he possess an excellent speaking voice, but he once demonstrated his ability to handle a feature role with flair. In 1777, John McKinly, President (governor) of Delaware, was captured by the British. Although Read was in Congress at the time, his position as Speaker of the Delaware Assembly necessitated a return to his state to act as governor. He and his family were crossing the Delaware River on their way home when their boat was intercepted by a British naval patrol. The Reads covered their baggage to hide every sign of their identity and cheerfully greeted the suspicious English. So convincing was the Read portrayal of an intensely Loyalist family that the sailors helped them on their way, much encouraged to find that the King still had such devoted adherents in the rebellious Colonies. Of course, Mrs. Read must also receive feature billing in this little drama, but perhaps her stage presence was aided by the fact that her brother, George Ross, was a Pennsylvania signer of the Declaration.

Read's career was a distinguished one. In addition to signing both the Declaration and the Constitution, he served in the first Federal Senate, was a Judge of Admiralty, and the Chief Justice of Delaware. Maybe it was not a question of stubbornness after all; it just took him longer to make up his mind. When he did, the decision was final.

THOMAS MCKEAN
Delaware

March 19, 1734   *June 24, 1817*

If it was hard to tell whether Thomas McKean (pronounced *McKane*) was from Delaware or Pennsylvania, it was equally difficult to decide whether he was a Federalist or a Democrat. Actually, he was a bit of each, occasionally even at the same time. But there was never any doubt about his position on independence. He was unswervingly for that. In fact it was he who fetched Caesar Rodney all the way from Dover to Philadelphia just to guarantee that Delaware would vote in favor of independence on July 2, 1776.

As far as state affiliation goes. McKean was born and raised in Pennsylvania, but entered law practice in Delaware. After his second marriage (1774) he moved to Philadelphia, but was elected to Congress from Delaware. He advanced in both states, presiding for 22 years (1777-1799) as Pennsylvania's Chief Justice while continuing to serve in Delaware at various times as Congressman, acting governor, and Speaker of the Assembly. McKean presided briefly over Congress in 1781, and in October of that year, had the pleasure of receiving General Washington's official notice of the British surrender at Yorktown.

If nobody was ever quite sure which state McKean called home, his political allegiances were even less clear. His fervent early enthusiasm for independence was worthy of Sam Adams, but when Pennsylvania adopted its Constitution in 1776, McKean thought it was democratic to the point of chaos. He moved into the Federalist camp, therefore, and stayed there until the publication of the Jay Treaty in 1795. Then, in indignation over the numerous concessions to the English, he went back to the Democrats. In 1799, after being elected governor of Pennsylvania as a Democrat, one of his first acts was to dismiss Federalist office holders and replace them with faithful members of his own party. Six years later McKean was elected governor again. By this time, however, he had broken with the Jeffersonians over their uncritical toleration of French insults. Naturally, he unceremoniously ousted the Democrats and replaced them with loyal Federalists.

Despite his frequent shifts of viewpoint and his bi-state affiliation, McKean was unfailingly loyal to America. He was unpredictable but honest, headstrong but sincere, a tough politician but an affectionate parent. On the whole, a complex but colorful Founding Father.

SAMUEL CHASE
Maryland

April 17, 1741   *June 19, 1811*

Samuel Chase habitually lived at the center of a storm. His hot temper, reckless nature, and keen thirst for conflict assured him an army of friends and foes, ever ready to fight over any conceivable issue. In all probability, Chase was the most combative man in Congress in 1776, and the most uncompromising revolutionary after Sam Adams himself. Chase's character, in the eyes of Tory Maryland, was pungently depicted by the mayor of Annapolis who called him a "busy, restless incendiary, a ringleader of mobs, a foul-mouthed and inflaming son of discord."

Like many high-spirited, impetuous people, Chase was a tireless worker. In 1777, he was a member of 21 Congressional committees and in 1778, 30. But perhaps Chase's most valuable burst of energy was his frenzied effort in 1776 to get Maryland to alter the instructions to its delegates in Congress. Chase wanted to vote for severing all ties with England, but his instructions forbade it. Not easily thwarted, he rode from Philadelphia to Annapolis and there, with Charles Carroll of Carrollton, fought doggedly until he had gained the state's consent to independence. Back from Annapolis to Philadelphia rode the jubilant Chase, the new instructions in his saddlebags. The ride was not quite so dramatic as Caesar Rodney's, but it was much longer and every bit as significant. It must also have been notably noisier, considering the comparative temperaments of the two horsemen.

Samuel Chase's subsequent career was full of ups and downs. In 1778 he fell into disfavor when he was accused of trying to corner the American flour market in order to sell at a huge profit to the French fleet. Even worse was his behavior as a justice of the United States Supreme Court in trying a sedition case in 1803. His version of a charge to the jury was a scathing denunciation of the defendants. Such judicial misconduct led to his impeachment during the Jefferson administration, although he was subsequently acquitted.

It is difficult to be an unqualified admirer of Samuel Chase. Hot-headedness, imprudence, and occasional self-seeking mar his image. An opponent referred to him as having more learning and knowledge than judgment; a friend spoke of him as abounding in good humor. History indicates he was a man of human weakness, on occasion great, but certainly a significant participant in one of humanity's great achievements, the Declaration of Independence.

WILLIAM PACA
Maryland

October 31, 1740   *October 13, 1799*

In general, two groups of Marylanders were identifiable by the early 1770's, an era of vigorous reaction to the poll tax supporting the Anglican clergy. Future American patriots were against it; future Tories were for it. William Paca's conspicuous opposition marked him as a coming leader in the struggle for independence. His fellow signers, Samuel Chase and Charles Carroll, could likewise have been identified as future patriots. It should be pointed out that Paca's opposition to the clergy tax stemmed from no anti-religious frame of mind. Later, as governor of his state, he advocated generous public assistance to *all* religious denominations. He opposed the poll tax simply because he saw it as a device for enforcing English domination of a nation he believed should be free.

The earliest Pacas may have been Italian, but if so, the line of descent has long been lost in the mists of English history. The family was, in any case, well established in America by Revolutionary times. Paca was typical of many of his patriot contemporaries. A successful lawyer, his means afforded him sufficient leisure for acquiring the graceful virtues of culture and civility. He served capably in the Maryland Provincial Legislature and in both Continental Congresses. Strongly influenced by the dynamic Samuel Chase, Paca early began resisting the growing assertion of British power in America. Like most of his colleagues, he was no real revolutionary, and in peaceful times would have been a notably quiet citizen. But the 1770s were not peaceful times, and when the Revolution came Paca's response was far from subdued. He, like others, equipped militia companies out of his own pocket, thus severely reducing the cash reserves with which he would face the depression that closely followed the Revolution.

Paca's public life included, in addition to three terms as Governor of Maryland, service in his state's Convention to ratify the Federal Constitution (1788), and ten years as a Federal District Judge (1789-1799). He died at his home, Wye Hall, in Talbot County, and was buried on his land in the rolling farm country of Maryland's Eastern Shore.

THOMAS STONE
Maryland

? 1743   *October 5, 1787*

Thomas Stone passed quietly through the turbulent early years of this country's life, making only ripples in the political waters of his time. Although by 1776 he had a dozen years of law practice and public life behind him—years marked by fierce controversy between Maryland's patriots and Tories—there was little independence fever in him. In fact, he actually favored the 1774 poll tax to support the Anglican clergy, a measure bitterly opposed by the other Maryland signers, and advocated treating for peace with Lord Howe in September 1776, a move viewed as subversive by many supporters of independence.

Perhaps it was simply the man's temperament that made him shy away from violent controversy. Certain qualities make good rebels but poor nation-builders, while other traits make reluctant revolutionaries but constructive statesmen. Very likely it was the possession of these latter capacities that won Stone a place on the joint Maryland-Virginia commission studying jurisdiction over Chesapeake Bay.

A visit to Port Tobacco, once the area of Thomas Stone's residence, gives a clue, but only a clue, to his quiet strength. The silent countryside may well have helped to make him the kind of man he was, although Stone had also lived in busy Annapolis before even building his residence, Habre de Venture.

We now possess only sparse knowledge of the events of Stone's life. Yet one personal detail comes through with great clarity. This signer was exceptionally devoted to his wife. In 1787 Maryland named Stone to the Constitutional Convention in Philadelphia. The choice was natural, for Stone had been a member of the committee that framed the earlier Articles of Confederation. But the appointment came at a poor time. Stone's wife lay seriously ill from an unsuccessful attempt to immunize her against smallpox. He declined the appointment in order to stay with her. When Mrs. Stone died, neither Maryland nor America held any further appeal for him, and he resolved to go to England.

While waiting at Alexandria, Virginia, for his ship to sail, Stone himself died, just a few months after his wife. His quiet career was over at 44 and he was laid to rest in the peaceful earth of rural Maryland.

CHARLES CARROLL
Maryland

September 19, 1737   *November 14, 1832*

There were so many Charles Carrolls in Maryland in 1776 that our signer was assured King George would not know which one of them to hang as a traitor. Carroll therefore added "of Carrollton" to his signature so that there could be no doubt about his identity. The story, although probably fictitious, could be true because Charles Carroll of Carrollton always had the courage to accept responsibility for his acts. Charles was born into a prominent Annapolis family. Because his Catholic faith severely limited his opportunities in Maryland, he went to Europe for his education. There he remained until he was 28, studying in Belgium, France and England.

Once back in America, however, he soon made his presence felt in the fight for independence. In 1773 he entered a spirited newspaper controversy with the gifted Tory, Daniel Dulany, over the tax to support the Anglican clergy. This issue arose in other Colonies, but in Maryland it had a special flavor. Founded by English Catholics as a haven of religious liberty, this Colony had seen its early rights chipped away, bit by bit, as the power of England became ever more oppressive. To many, the clergy tax was a hated symbol of lost religious freedom. Early in the Revolution Congress tried to put Carroll's religion and his command of the French language to good diplomatic use. Though not even a member of Congress, he accompanied Benjamin Franklin and Samuel Chase on a mission to seek French Canadian support for the American cause.

Despite the failure of this effort Carroll made a profound impression on Franklin, and was shortly after elected to Congress himself. But this wealthy Marylander spent little time in public office. He did serve in his state legislature for a while, and briefly as a Senator in the First Congress. Far more of his time was devoted to managing his extensive lands and such business interests as the Chesapeake and Ohio Canal Company and the Baltimore and Ohio Railroad. One strong expression of his views on public issues came during the War of 1812, which he denounced as unnecessary, senseless and immoral.

This gentle, courageous man had one memorable distinction. He outlived all the other signers, dying in 1832 at the age of 95. His long life had been basically quiet, but Carroll had known how to show heroism when the situation called for it.

GEORGE WYTHE
Virginia

1726   *June 8, 1806*

George Wythe never fought a battle, coined a memorable phrase, or immortalized himself as a popular hero. Yet, during his sixty years as a lawyer, his impact on American history was enormous. It was not only what he did himself but what he brought out of others.

Naming a few of his one-time law students makes this point clear. Thomas Jefferson, John Marshall, James Monroe, and Henry Clay would constitute an impressive alumni roster for any law school, let alone for one teacher.

George Wythe (pronounced *with*) was the unchallenged leader of Virginia's jurists for over thirty years. He was also the first professor of law in America, occupying that position at William and Mary College from 1779 to 1790.

Yet, one aspect of Wythe's career led to an irony without parallel among our Founding Fathers. From 1776 to 1779 he, Thomas Jefferson, and Edmund Pendleton served as a committee to revise and update Virginia's laws. Although the revision was in general progressive, it contained two flaws which would later figure in the circumstances accompanying Wythe's death. One was a provision banning testimony by blacks against whites; the other was the lack of an adequate forgery law.

Wythe, although twice married, had no surviving children. He had therefore, hopefully if unwisely, selected his grandnephew, George W. Sweeney, as his chief heir. Sweeney was an unprincipled spendthrift who by 1806 had piled up a staggering load of debts. In April of that year he forged his great-uncle's name to six checks. A desperate effort to cover up these crimes and collect his inheritance seems to have driven Sweeney to the fearful extreme of poisoning Wythe's coffee on the morning of May 25. The old man lived on in agony for two weeks, dying on June 8.

Sweeney was arraigned for the murder on June 23. But the charge collapsed at the trial, mainly because, as the *Richmond Enquirer* put it, "It was gleaned from the evidence of negroes which is not permitted to go against a white man." The chief prosecution witness, Wythe's black housekeeper, could not testify against the white Sweeney. Even Sweeney's subsequent conviction of forgery fell through because in 1806 Virginia had no law covering forgeries involving corporations, in this case the Bank of Virginia.

Who could have foreseen in 1776 that Virginia's greatest lawyer, in revising his state's laws, would overlook the two that applied most directly to his own last days?

George Wythe

RICHARD HENRY LEE
Virginia

January 20, 1732   *June 19, 1794*

Some of those who signed the Declaration of Independence did so almost accidentally. They just happened to be in Congress when the document was presented for signatures. Not so with Richard Henry Lee. On June 7, 1776 he himself introduced the resolutions which called for a final severing of America's political ties with Great Britain. Lee might almost be considered the father of American independence.

This great leader came from a well known and wealthy Virginia family that had contributed many notable early leaders to the

Colony and would continue to produce great Americans long after the Revolution. He was born in 1732, about a month before George Washington, and was educated first at the ancestral home, Stratford, and later in England. Elected to the Virginia House of Burgesses in 1758, he soon showed himself far too liberal for the taste of most other members of his social class. For instance, he introduced a bill to stop the importation of slaves into Virginia, and he denounced Treasurer John Robinson for what was eventually shown to be a thoroughly dishonest handling of the Colony's funds. As far as the aristocrats were concerned, Richard Henry Lee was a bit of a nuisance.

George III felt the same way, for Lee forcefully opposed the Stamp Act of 1765 and led an association of prominent Westmoreland County residents in a boycott of English goods until the act was repealed. But the King did not give up, and within a few years Lee was fighting enforcement of the Townshend Acts, urging the formation of Committees of Correspondence, and cooperating with Patrick Henry in moving Virginia toward a final separation from Great Britain.

If the King found Lee a nuisance, there were others who felt differently. Inscribed on his tombstone is the epitaph "We cannot do without you." Although he opposed the Federal Constitution of 1787, and fought tirelessly to prevent its adoption, he became a Senator in the First Congress and led the movement to adopt a Bill of Rights. Perhaps the writer of Lee's epitaph had this in mind. Surely the Bill of Rights is a heritage from Richard Henry Lee that we would not want to be without.

Richard Henry Lee

THOMAS JEFFERSON
Virginia

April 13, 1743   *July 4, 1826*

Thomas Jefferson stepped onto the stage of history at just the right time. His ideals were the ideals of the Revolution. His pen incorporated them into the Declaration of Independence. His influence helped assure their survival in the new nation. He concisely expressed the spirit of independence when he swore "eternal hostility against every form of tyranny over the mind of man." To understand Jefferson is to grasp the essence of the American ideal.

This great Virginian was born in the up-country of his state, far back from the coast. Important Virginians, as everybody knew, came from the Tidewater, but young Thomas had one thing going for him anyway: his mother was a Randolph. A Randolph, even from the upcountry, was a power to be reckoned with.

The future President's education was much like that of other moderately wealthy Virginians, but his intellect was not. He eagerly read the classics, acquired an intense interest in science, perfected his musical talents, and absorbed the best thoughts of ancient and modern political thinkers.

Jefferson frequently drew on this great storehouse in later years. When British prisoners were held in Virginia, he joined the musically gifted ones in performing string quartets. Letters to his friends were rich in Latin and Greek quotations. While Minister to France he shipped grains and fruit trees to America in an effort to improve its agriculture. He even bested the French naturalist Georges Buffon in a controversy over the size of North American mammals. The Frenchman never recovered from the mass of scientific data under which Jefferson buried him.

Combined with this great mind was a warm, sensitive humanity. His affection for his wife and two daughters was a moving example of human love at its best. His wife's death in 1782 and his younger daughter's in 1804 were shattering blows that nearly cost him his reason. But he carried on, drawing ever closer to his remaining daughter and her family.

Thomas Jefferson was the right man in the right place at the right time. Even his departure from life came at the right moment, July 4, 1826, the 50th anniversary of independence. He and crusty old John Adams took leave of life on the same day, each comforted by the illusion that the other still lived. It was a passing of giants.

BENJAMIN HARRISON
Virginia

? 1726

April 24, 1791

Benjamin Harrison was a portly, jovial member of one of Virginia's best families. Almost everybody of importance in that colony seems to have been related to him either by blood or by marriage. For instance, his first cousin, Carter Braxton, was a fellow signer of the Declaration.

But Harrison was a man of ability as well as influence, who skillfully operated extensive agricultural and shipping interests from "Berkeley," his stately James River plantation. A reluctant rebel at first, he had become a solidly established patriot leader by the time of his election to Congress in 1775. So highly respected was he that Congress named him chairman of its Committee of the Whole, the parliamentary arrangement for facilitating informal discussion at a time of critical debate. Although no resolutions could be passed in this committee, the most significant debates on independence occurred there, presided over by the capable Virginian.

Harrison did not lose interest in the newly independent America after he left Congress in 1777. In 1781, as Governor of Virginia, he presided over the cession of his state's western land claims to the Federal Government. This was an extremely important event, for it subordinated a large state to the authority of the emerging national government. Such actions by Virginia and several other states were indispensable preliminaries to the development of a workable Federal Constitution six years later.

There is something appealing about good-humored Benjamin Harrison. Despite the fearful experience of having his father and two small sisters killed by lightning, an event that would deprive many men of the capacity to see the light side of things, Harrison always retained the ability to joke. One exercise of his wit was, literally, gallows humor. He is reported to have taunted scrawny Elbridge Gerry, not renowned for his sense of humor, about the problem of being too light for a good hanging by the British. As Harrison saw it, a big man would soon be dispatched, but Gerry might kick and squirm on the rope all day long.

Some families have woven themselves deeply into the fabric of American history. The Adamses, for instance, and the Lees. But Benjamin Harrison is the only Founding Father who had both a son and a great grandson become presidents. This signer left an impression like few others on his country's future.

Benj Harrison

THOMAS NELSON, JR.
Virginia

December 26, 1738   *January 4, 1789*

John Adams, great as he was, had an unpleasant knack for noticing everything about a man except what was really important. He thus dismissed Thomas Nelson as "a fat man who is a speaker, and alert and lively for his weight." There is no mention that Nelson was a dynamic advocate of independence, an openhanded contributor to the support of Virginia troops, and a wealthy landholder who had staked all his properties and assets on the dubious chance of America's winning the Revolution. Adams also missed the fact that in May 1776 Nelson introduced into the Virginia legislature a resolution urging

Congress to declare independence. Once the legislature approved this proposal, Nelson himself, extra weight and all, carried the demand to Congress.

There is no doubt that Thomas Nelson was bulky, but he could move fast when he had to. A fine illustration of this was his aggressive assumption of the governorship of Virginia in the spring of 1781. His predecessor, Thomas Jefferson, had experienced a dismal term in office that ended with Virginia in a state of acute military unpreparedness. Nelson wasted no time and omitted no sacrifices in rectifying the situation. His vigor paid off handsomely. When Cornwallis backed himself into a corner at Yorktown, Nelson's hometown, the ponderous General was there with 3,000 men, poised for the kill. His conduct and that of his troops earned high praise from General Washington after the final victory.

Nelson resembled other patriots like Robert Morris and William Paca in unstintingly expending his resources on the troops. But he did something nobody else did. He ordered his own house bombarded in order to drive out British officers who assumed it would be spared during the fierce shelling of Yorktown.

Thomas Nelson gave everything he had to the winning of independence and it left him devastated in both health and resources. Badgered by creditors and petty critics, he moved from Yorktown to a small home in Hanover County, northwest of Richmond. There he died, wracked by asthma, at the age of fifty, one of the Revolution's authentic heroes.

FRANCIS LIGHTFOOT LEE
Virginia.

October 14, 1734   *January 11, 1797*

The Lees of Virginia were a remarkable family and their home, "Stratford," was unique for the number of great Americans whose lives began there. Richard Henry Lee, mover of the resolutions for independence, was one of them, as was his less renowned but hardly less gifted brother, Francis Lightfoot Lee. In a later generation "Stratford" also saw the birth of Robert E. Lee, the great Confederate general.

Francis Lee's pre-Revolutionary political career included nearly two decades of service in the Virginia House of Burgesses

(1758-1776). He was an early supporter of the American cause, including the Westmoreland Association (1766) sponsored by his brother, and the Virginia Committee of Correspondence (1773). But active as he was, this patriot was quiet, unspectacular, and relatively unvocal. For these reasons Francis was largely overshadowed during the Revolution by his dramatic older brother. In one way, however, the younger man more than held his own. He possessed a superb singing voice that made him much in demand at social gatherings.

The Lees illustrate one of the curious ways in which circumstances could realign families during the Revolution. Another older brother, William, resided in England and was sheriff of London while the war raged on. He rendered valuable service as an unofficial American "listening post" without at any time forfeiting the confidence of either side.

Although Francis Lee was never as influential as Richard Henry, the younger brother had a mind of his own. When the Federal Constitution was proposed for ratification in 1788 Francis stood strongly for it, in contrast to Richard's unyielding opposition.

With the return of peace, Francis Lee retired from the public arena and lived inconspicuously on his small plantation "Menokin." He died of pleurisy in the fall of 1797, leaving no children, but bequeathing to all Americans his solid contribution to the liberty of their nation.

Francis Lightfoot Lee

CARTER BRAXTON
Virginia

September 10, 1736   *October 10, 1797*

Carter Braxton, a first cousin of signer Benjamin Harrison, had a hard time during the Revolution. For one thing, his prosperity as a planter disappeared with the loss of his British markets. Further, his efforts to compensate for this setback by investing heavily in commercial shipping proved disastrous when the British Navy swept American merchantmen from the seas.

But Braxton had a problem even more fundamental than his economic woes. A born peacemaker, he long retained his faith that the British-American dispute could be peacefully resolved.

He had opposed Parliament by his support of Richard Henry Lee's resolutions of 1769 asserting that Virginia alone had the right to tax Virginians. Yet Braxton really did not belong with Lee. Related by marriage to John Robinson, the target of Lee's corruption charges in 1765, Braxton was a conservative blueblood who bristled under such assaults on the privileged class. There is something admirable about this signer's persistent, if naive, loyalty to his aristocratic friends, even though it long kept him in opposition to Virginia giants like Jefferson and Patrick Henry.

Braxton served only about a year in Congress (1776), reluctantly agreeing to independence and signing the Declaration. He continued active in his state's affairs for another decade, but seems never to have resigned himself completely to the bloody conflict he had always regarded as avoidable. His last years were darkened by an inability to recover from the grave financial losses he had incurred during the Revolution. He died hopelessly in debt despite the efforts of several of his sons to pay his bills. Two details of Braxton's life are of some interest. He sired eighteen children, two by his first wife and sixteen by his second. In this respect he was literally a founding father. Finally, despite diligent research by some of his descendants, no one today knows where Carter Braxton is buried. Never quite comfortable with his situation in the Revolution, he has not found his rightful place even in death.

Carter Braxton

WILLIAM HOOPER
North Carolina

June 28, 1742   *October 14, 1790*

Boston in the 1760s was a hard place for a young lawyer to make a living. There were too many attorneys there already. William Hooper, fresh from his studies under James Otis, was acutely aware of that. Therefore, like many other New Englanders, Hooper moved south in order to begin his profession where there was a realistic chance of success. He opened his practice in 1764 in Wilmington, North Carolina.

It did not take long for Hooper to rise politically and socially in his new environment. After marrying into a prominent Carolina family, he used his considerable personal and professional qualities to win election to the state legislature. He seemed solidly installed as a rising member of the ruling class.

In late 1770 a backcountry rebellion broke out against the dominance of the eastern coastal aristocracy. This uprising, called the War of the Regulation, pitted unpropertied citizens from the western part of the colony against the landed gentry from the east. Hooper, a Loyalist then, fought against these "Regulators" as a member of Governor Tryon's expedition in the spring of 1771.

How drastically the picture was to change! As British oppression of the Colonies increased, Hooper became a leading defender of American rights. Both his and his wife's families remained Loyalist, but Hooper eloquently advocated resistance. Surprisingly, perhaps, many of the Regulators, once bitter foes of the established authority, now aligned themselves with King George. Rebels and Loyalists had switched sides.

Hooper suffered greatly from the war, frequently being forced to endure prolonged separations from his wife and children. On several occasions he was forced to flee to avoid capture. His home and possessions in Wilmington were destroyed, and it was not until 1782 that he was able to rejoin his family permanently in their new residence at Hillsboro. By that time he had only a few years to live. The war had so drained his strength and depleted his finances that he died prematurely in 1790 at the age of 48.

John Adams admired Hooper and considered him one of the finest speakers in Congress. The statue over Hooper's burial place near Greensboro shows him driving a point home with oratorical vigor. But the real proof of Hooper's mettle was the sacrifices he made in the cause of American freedom. His old mentor, James Otis, would have been proud of him.

JOSEPH HEWES
North Carolina

January 23, 1730   *November 10, 1779*

Eighteenth Century Edenton, a pleasant little port on the North Carolina coast, could sometimes be anything but quiet. Frequently during the last years before the Revolution it became thoroughly upset. It had its own "tea party," its own nonimportation agreement, and its own active part in the North Carolina Committee of Correspondence. Edenton might have been pleasant, but it was not going to tolerate any violations of the rights of its people.

A major force behind this strong stand was a little man who, like the town itself, was usually, but not always, quiet. Joseph Hewes, a native of New Jersey, had come to Edenton about 1763 and set up an importing business there. By the 1770s he was generally regarded as the town's leading citizen.

Hewes was elected to both Continental Congresses where he worked tirelessly to remove the causes of American discontent. At first, separation from England was not his idea of the solution at all. But his patience, like Edenton's, had its limits. They were finally reached during the heated Congressional debates on independence, when no conciliatory offer came from Great Britain. It seemed to many, including John Adams, that the Colonies were about equally divided on the question: six for, six against, North Carolina doubtful. Since Hewes was the only delegate from his state then in Congress, his vote was vital. Let John Adams describe the moment of decision: "Mr. Hewes, who had hitherto constantly voted against it [independence], started upright, and lifting up both hands to heaven cried out, 'It is done! And I will abide by it.' " The quiet man's patience had run out.

Once committed to independence, Hewes labored feverishly to make it a reality. His work as chairman of the naval committee of Congress was outstanding, one of its notable achievements being the commissioning of John Paul Jones in the Continental Navy.

Unhappily, Hewes did not live to see the final victory. His conscientiousness kept him at work day and night for weeks on end. His health, never robust, gave out under the strain, and he died in Philadelphia, still on the job. Hewes was a quiet man who stood at a turning of the road of history, pointing out the hard route to freedom.

Joseph Hewes,

JOHN PENN
North Carolina

May 17, 1740   *September 14, 1788*

The Declaration of Independence did not hit the world like an unheralded thunderbolt. It was preceded by small-scale declarations from Suffolk County, Massachusetts in 1774, and from Mecklenburg County, North Carolina in 1775. On April 12, 1776 the North Carolina Provincial Congress promulgated the Halifax Resolves supporting in advance any move Congress might make towards separation from Great Britain. One month later, Virginia echoed the same views in even more strident tones. A lot of heat had been applied to the kettle of rebellion before it boiled over in July, 1776. John Penn, a native of Caroline County,

Virginia, figured prominently in the Halifax Resolves. Sooner than his colleagues, Hooper and Hewes, he had grasped the banner of revolution. Although trained for the law by cautious, conservative Edmund Pendleton of Virginia, Penn showed scant hesitation about advocating independence.

This signer had a slow start in life. Barely literate at the age of 18, he applied himself diligently to study, principally in Pendleton's extensive library. He progressed rapidly enough to begin reading law under the same mentor. His desire for advancement in the legal profession induced him to move in 1774 to North Carolina where the competition was less formidable. Penn, a member of the North Carolina Provincial Congress of 1775, went to Congress in the same year, and from then until 1780 shuttled back and forth between state and national legislatures. In 1780 he was outstanding for his success in raising militia to oppose the movement of Cornwallis's army through the state. His efforts were triumphantly crowned by the American victories at King's Mountain and the Cowpens.

After the war, Penn left public life mainly because his wholehearted devotion to the American cause had ruined him financially. He did not survive the Revolution very long. Like the other two North Carolina signers, he died in his late forties, physically ravaged by the ordeal of war. Although a lesser figure among the Founding Fathers, John Penn gave the American cause his unfailing best. No man could do more.

John Penn

EDWARD RUTLEDGE
South Carolina

November 23, 1749   *January 23, 1800*

Edward Rutledge drove John Adams nearly crazy. The zealous New Englander, full of a passion for independence, wanted action from Congress. He begged, pleaded, threatened, and promised, but for a long time he could not get quite what he wanted. Rutledge was one of the reasons. Although the youngest man in Congress, this gifted 26-year old had assumed leadership of the South Carolina delegation, and they were just not ready for independence when Adams was.

Rutledge's credentials as a patriot were solid. He had been

educated in England, but upon his return to South Carolina in 1773 he promptly took up the cause of the Colonies. He served in both Continental Congresses and in the South Carolina legislature, and was captured by the British when they occupied his native Charleston in 1780.

Most of this was unknown to Adams, of course; all he could see in early 1776 was a brash young Southerner blocking a declaration of independence.

Rutledge had his reasons for this reluctance, but mulish stubbornness was not one of them. He was convinced that the Colonies had little chance of survival unless they formed a united government *before* they proclaimed their independence. It was not so much that he opposed independence as that he wanted it to have the best possible chance of success.

History proved Adams right and Rutledge wrong, but the Carolinian was a good loser. When independence became inevitable, and he was assured that it would be agreeable to the citizens of his state, he swung his delegation over for the sake of unanimity. Nothing in his subsequent life indicated there was anything shallow or insincere about this change of position.

Edward Rutledge was well liked and highly respected by his peers. As he grew older he put on weight and became gouty, but continued to hold public office. In 1798 he was elected governor of his state, but failed to survive the two-year term. On January 23, 1800, at the age of 50, he died suddenly, much beloved and greatly mourned.

THOMAS HEYWARD, JR.
South Carolina

July 28, 1746

March 6, 1809

Thomas Heyward now lies in the old family cemetery, his burial place marked by both its original monument and a commemorative column erected later by the state of South Carolina. The old house has long been gone, but the stately moss-draped oaks must all have been there in Heyward's times. In the heat of a summer day one can still imagine the sights and sounds of the old plantation. But everything is quiet now.

The other Heyward house is different. It is located in downtown Charleston where the pace is brisk and the people busy. The tranquillity of Old House and the activity of the city reflected closely the contrasts of Thomas Heyward's life. Part of it was spent in the quiet world of the plantation, the library, and the study; but another part of it was spent amid the turmoil of debate and the clash of battle.

Like the other three South Carolina signers, Heyward studied law in England. Not only was this considered good professional training, but residence in the mother country was a distinct status symbol among South Carolina aristocrats.

At 25 Heyward was back in Carolina engaged in legal practice. At 26 he was a member of the Provincial Assembly. In 1776 he served on the Committee of Eleven drafting a constitution for the state of South Carolina. His Congressional years (1776-1778) preceded a period of military service that ended in 1780. At that time he, Edward Rutledge, and Arthur Middleton were captured at Charleston and sent to St. Augustine as British prisoners. While in the Castillo de San Marcos, Heyward composed a parody of "God Save the King" which he called "God Save the States." It is unlikely that its cleverness particularly impressed his captors.

During his imprisonment Heyward's estate was plundered by the British, but an even more harrowing ordeal occurred on his way home after being released. Somehow he fell overboard and escaped drowning only by hanging on to the rudder until he could be hauled safely aboard.

Heyward founded the South Carolina Agricultural Society in 1785, and his last public involvement was probably at the convention of 1790 that wrote a new state constitution.

The cycle ended in 1809 where it had begun in 1746, and Thomas Heyward returned to the great oaks he had once known so well.

THOMAS LYNCH, JR.
South Carolina

August 5, 1749   *? 1779*

The story of Thomas Lynch is a sad one, mainly because it is so short. Yet Lynch gave himself as fully to the American cause as did John Adams, Thomas Jefferson, or Benjamin Franklin. It was simply that he had so little time in which to make his contribution.

Thomas Lynch, Jr. had studied law in England and served in various legislative bodies in pre-revolutionary South Carolina. Fundamentally, though, he was a planter. If the Revolution had not come along, he would probably have passed his days growing rice and enjoying a life of cultured leisure.

But the Revolution did come along and Lynch was prepared to do his part. In 1775, while serving as captain in the First South Carolina Regiment, he contracted what was called "bilious fever." Was it malaria? Yellow fever? We cannot say now, but the effect terribly weakened him for the rest of his brief life.

While young Lynch had been in military service, his father, Thomas Sr., was in Congress. Early in 1776 the father suffered a stroke that severely limited his ability to serve effectively. Despite his own fragile health, the son was also sent to Philadelphia as a delegate. There was little for him to do but sign the Declaration before the state of his father's health made an immediate return to South Carolina imperative. The ailing father and son began the long homeward journey, but only one of them completed it. Thomas Lynch, Sr. died at Annapolis, Maryland, hundreds of miles from his home, and his son had no choice but to bury him there.

The rest of the story is brief. The young man's health grew steadily worse. In 1779, he and his wife set sail for the West Indies, hoping to change ships there for the healthier climate of southern France. What happened we will never know, for their ship disappeared completely, without a trace or a survivor.

Thus Thomas Lynch, a signer of the Declaration of Independence at 27, was dead at 30. It is sad that he had so few years and so little health with which to enjoy America's independence.

Thomas Lynch Jun

ARTHUR MIDDLETON
South Carolina

June 26, 1742   *January 1, 1787*

Middleton Place near Charleston still looks out on the graceful Ashley River. Its once busy fields are quiet now, but the view remains incomparable. It is difficult to visualize a high-spirited rebel coming from so tranquil a place. Arthur Middleton was a younger son of one of South Carolina's great 18th century families. Educated in England at Cambridge, he studied law in London, and toured the Continent. He also returned to live in England from 1768 to 1771. One would have expected him to develop into a loyal defender of the rights of Parliament and King George III. But Middleton was neither a calm nor a submissive man. After his return to South Carolina in 1771 he entered the Assembly and took his place among the zealous patriot leaders. He became active on South Carolina's Committee of Safety and, in April 1776, participated in the seizure of powder and weapons from the public storehouses in Charleston.

A curious feature of the South Carolina Congressional delegation that signed the Declaration of Independence was the extreme youth of its members. Two were in their twenties (Rutledge and Lynch), Heyward was 30, and Middleton at 34 was the oldest of this group of younger sons sent to Congress while their fathers and older brothers stayed in Charleston to tend to the apparently more important task of building a state government. In 1780 Charleston fell to the British under Cornwallis, and its garrison became prisoners of war. Every South Carolina signer except Thomas Lynch, by then dead, was in the captured city. They were shipped to the prison of Castillo de San Marcos at St. Augustine, Florida, returning only at the end of the war.

For Arthur Middleton there was little time left after coming back to Middleton Place. He served briefly in Congress (1781-1782), but for the most part devoted his last years to the life of a planter, including such passions of his as hunting and horse racing. This signer died on New Year's Day in 1787, probably of malaria. He was buried in one of the most secluded of Middleton Place's many restful corners: a quiet repose at the end of a brief but turbulent life.

BUTTON GWINNETT
Georgia

? 1735   *May 16, 1777*

Some men make good rebels. People with hot tempers, critical minds, and small concern for the feelings of others often possess a reckless indifference to the consequences of their actions. These qualities are helpful in promoting revolutions, but they inevitably make bitter personal enemies. This was Button Gwinnett's problem.

Gwinnett was born in England. His odd first name was given in honor of his godmother Barbara Button, a cousin of his mother. Before leaving England, he had married and entered the export business. In 1765, when about 30, he crossed the Atlantic and settled in Savannah. At first he resumed his career as a merchant, but later purchased St. Catherine's Island off the Georgia cost and took up the life of a planter.

In the years just before the Revolution Gwinnett came much under the influence of Lyman Hall and the New England group that had settled at Sunbury. They were as hot for independence as was old Sam Adams. Gwinnett's naturally ardent nature took up the cause with such enthusiasm that even Hall called him "a Whig to excess." This was the beginning of trouble.

At best, Gwinnett was regarded as a latecomer by older Georgians. Aligning himself with the New England group made matters worse. Although he was elected to Congress in 1776 and voted for independence, he made many enemies. Most implacable were the McIntoshes of Savannah. When Gwinnett became governor of Georgia in 1777 he was ordered by Congress to arrest George McIntosh on suspicion of treason. Nothing could have pleased Gwinnett more. A proposed expedition against the British forts in Florida, under the command of George's brother, General Lachlan McIntosh, was badly bungled, partly due to Gwinnett's officious meddling in the chain of command. Recriminations flew back and forth, a challenge was issued, a duel fought. Both McIntosh and Gwinnett were wounded, but the latter's wounds proved fatal. He thus died at the hands of a bitter personal enemy less than a year after signing the Declaration.

There is a final irony in the case of this Founding Father. He is now remembered among the signers mainly for a trivial reason: his autograph is the rarest and most valuable of all.

Button Gwinnett

LYMAN HALL
Georgia

April 12, 1724   *October 19, 1790*

Sir James Wright, royal governor of Georgia in 1775, did not particularly care for the citizens of Sunbury. He accused them of being "of the Puritan independent sect" and of retaining "a strong tincture of Republican principles." Especially singled out by Sir James was "Lyman Hall, of New England extract," one of a number of "insignificant fanatics." Dr. Lyman Hall was neither insignificant nor fanatic. Born in Wallingford, Connecticut, he began his career as a minister. After some unhappy experiences in that profession, however, he turned to medicine and in 1758 moved to Sunbury, Georgia, a town populated almost exclusively by families of New England origin. In a region filled with malaria and yellow fever there was plenty of need for Dr. Hall's professional services. But Hall was involved with these former New Englanders in more than a professional way. He fully shared their ambitions for independence, and was elected their delegate to provincial meetings in nearby Savannah in 1774 and 1775. These gatherings did not strike enough sparks for independence, however, and the patriots failed for a time to bring Georgia into line with the other Colonies in the struggle for freedom. The best Sunbury could do at first was to send Dr. Hall to Congress as a sort of observer. He did not become fully accredited until July 4, 1775, several months later.

While Lyman Hall was not one of the towering giants of American independence, he certainly contributed significantly toward its attainment. His later career was equally creditable. Elected governor of Georgia in 1783, he devoted much effort to advancing the cause of education. His most notable achievement in this line was the establishment in 1784 of the University of Georgia. Lyman Hall took his New England spirit of liberty to Georgia and turned it into a powerful weapon in the Revolutionary struggle. But New England never entirely relinquished him. Though his body rests in Georgia, the old cemetery in Wallingford has a tombstone bearing his name and dedicated to his imperishable love of freedom.

Lyman Hall

GEORGE WALTON
Georgia

1741   *February 2, 1804*

George Walton, a native of Virginia, was a self-made man. He was orphaned as a small child, had little formal education, and served an apprenticeship to a carpenter. His unpromising beginnings make us think of signers like Roger Sherman and Samuel Huntington, also largely self-taught, who apprenticed as a shoemaker and a cooper respectively before the study of law opened up new possibilities for them.

Walton utilized this same gateway to success after moving to Savannah in 1769. He was admitted to the legal profession in

1774, at the same time taking up the cause of American independence. He quickly made a name for himself as a patriot, being repeatedly elected to Congress between 1776 and 1781, although frequently unable to attend the sessions in distant Philadelphia.

One of the low points in Walton's life was the fall of Savannah in 1778. Present as a Colonel of Militia, he was wounded during the battle for the city, and captured by the British. Lt. Col. Campbell, the victorious commander, treated him courteously, allowing him to give his parole until he had recovered from his wounds.

Afterwards Campbell tried a little bargaining for his prize prisoner. As a signer of the Declaration of Independence and a member of Congress, Walton seemed to Campbell to be worth at least a Brigadier General by way of exchange. However, Congress did not rate their colleague as highly as all that. They pointed out that he was only a Colonel and should be exchanged for no rank above his own. We wonder if Walton felt flattered by such reasoning. In any case, the exchange was eventually made for a British Naval Captain.

There is a rather informative point to be noted about Walton's political views. He was actually a conservative, and became more so as he grew older. His two fellow Georgia signers, Button Gwinnett and Lyman Hall, were far more radical. The American cause united men of vastly different political persuasions, despite the fact that probably no more than one third of all Americans ever actively supported the rebellion.

Walton's life after the war remained linked to the new nation's development. He was at various times Georgia's Chief Justice, Governor, and Senator, aligning himself with the Federalist party. He died in Augusta at his last home, College Hill.

Declaration of Independence

IN CONGRESS, JULY 4, 1776

The unanimous Declaration of the Thirteen united States of America,

When in the Course of human events, it becomes necessary for one people to dissolve the political bands which have connected them with another, and to assume among the Powers of the earth, the separate and equal station to which the Laws of Nature and of Nature's God entitle them, a decent respect to the opinions of mankind requires that they should declare the causes which impel them to the separation.

We hold these truths to be self-evident, that all men are created equal, that they are endowed by their Creator with certain unalienable Rights, that among these are Life, Liberty and the pursuit of Happiness. That to secure these rights, Governments are instituted among Men, deriving their just powers from the consent of the governed, That whenever any Form of Government becomes destructive of these ends, it is the Right of the People to alter or to abolish it, and to institute new Government, laying its foundation on such principles and organizing its powers in such form, as to them shall seem most likely to effect their Safety and Happiness. Prudence, indeed, will dictate that Governments long established should not be changed for light and transient causes; and accordingly all experience hath shown, that mankind are more disposed to suffer, while evils are sufferable, than to right themselves by abolishing the forms to which they are accustomed. But when a long train of abuses and usurpations, pursuing invariably the same Object evinces a design to reduce them under absolute Despotism, it is their right, it is their duty, to throw off such Government, and to provide new Guards for their future security.—Such has been the patient sufferance of these Colonies; and such is now the necessity which constrains them to alter their former Systems of Government. The history of the present King of Great Britain is a history of repeated injuries and usurpations, all having in direct object the establishment of an absolute Tyranny over these States. To prove this, let Facts be submitted to a candid world.

He has refused his Assent to Laws, the most wholesome and

necessary for the public good.

He has forbidden his Governors to pass Laws of immediate and pressing importance, unless suspended in their operation till his Assent should be obtained; and when so suspended, he has utterly neglected to attend to them.

He has refused to pass other Laws for the accommodation of large districts of people, unless those people would relinquish the right of Representation in the Legislature, a right inestimable to them and formidable to tyrants only.

He has called together legislative bodies at places unusual, uncomfortable, and distant from the depository of their Public Records, for the sole purpose of fatiguing them into compliance with his measures.

He has dissolved Representative Houses repeatedly, for opposing with manly firmness his invasions on the right of the people.

He has refused for a long time, after such dissolutions, to cause others to be elected; whereby the Legislative Powers, incapable of Annihilation, have returned to the People at large for their exercise; the State remaining in the mean time exposed to all the dangers of invasion from without, and convulsions within.

He has endeavored to prevent the population of these States; for that purpose obstructing the Laws for Naturalization of Foreigners; refusing to pass others to encourage their migrations hither, and raising the conditions of new Appropriations of Lands.

He has obstructed the Administration of Justice, by refusing his Assent to Laws for establishing Judiciary Powers.

He has made Judges dependent on his Will alone, for the tenure of their offices, and the amount and payment of their salaries.

He has erected a multitude of New Offices, and sent hither swarms of Officers to harass our people, and eat out their substance.

He has kept among us, in times of peace, Standing Armies without the Consent of our legislatures.

He has affected to render the Military independent of and superior to the Civil Power.

He has combined with others to subject us to a jurisdiction foreign to our constitution, and unacknowledged by our laws; giving his Assent to their acts of pretended Legislation:

For quartering large bodies of armed troops us:

For protecting them, by a mock Trial, from Punishment for any Murders which they should commit on the Inhabitants of these States:

For cutting off our Trade with all parts of the world:

For imposing taxes on us without our Consent:

For depriving us in many cases, of the benefits of Trail by Jury:

For transporting us beyond Seas to be tried for pretended offenses:

For abolishing the free System of English Laws in a neighboring Province, establishing therein an Arbitrary government, and enlarging its Boundaries so as to render it at once an example and fit instrument for introducing the same absolute rule into these Colonies:

For taking away our Charters, abolishing our most valuable Laws, and altering fundamentally the Forms of our Governments:

For suspending our own Legislatures, and declaring themselves invested with Power to legislate for us in all cases whatsoever.

He has abdicated Government here, by declaring us out of his Protection and waging War against us.

He has plundered our seas, ravaged our Coasts, burnt our towns, and destroyed the lives of our people.

He is at this time transporting large armies of foreign mercenaries to compleat the works of death, desolation and tyranny, already begun with circumstances of Cruelty & perfidy scarcely paralleled in the most barbarous ages, and totally unworthy the Head of a civilized nation.

He has constrained our fellow Citizens taken Captive on the high Seas to bear Arms against their Country, to become the executioners of their friends and Brethren, or to fall themselves by their Hands.

He has excited domestic insurrections amongst us, and has endeavored to bring on the inhabitants of our frontiers, the merciless Indian Savages, whose known rule of warfare, is an undistinguished destruction of all ages, sexes and conditions.

In every stage of these Oppressions We have Petitioned for Redress in the most humble terms: Our repeated Petitions have been answered only by repeated injury. A Prince, whose character is thus marked by every act which may define a Tyrant, is unfit to be the ruler of a free people.

Nor have We been wanting in attentions to our British brethren. We have warned them from time to time of attempts by their legislature to extend an unwarrantable jurisdiction over us. We have reminded them of the circumstances of our emigration and settlement here. We have appealed to their native justice and magnanimity, and we have conjured them by the ties of our common kindred to disavow these usurpations which, would inevitably interrupt our connections and correspondence. They too have been deaf to the voice of justice and of consanguinity. We must, therefore, acquiesce in the necessity, which denounces our Separation, and hold them, as we hold the rest of mankind, Enemies in War, in Peace Friends.

We, therefore, the Representatives of the united States of America, in General Congress, Assembled, appealing to the Supreme Judge of the world for the rectitude of our intentions, do, in the Name, and by authority of the good People of these Colonies, solemnly publish and declare, That these United Colonies are, and of Right ought to be Free and Independent States; that they are Absolved from all Allegiance to the British Crown, and that all political connection between them and the State of Great Britain, is and ought to be totally dissolved; and that as Free and Independent States, they have full power to levy War, conclude Peace, contract Alliances, establish Commerce, and to do all other Acts and Things which Independent States may of right do. And for the support of this Declaration, with a firm reliance on the Protection of Divine Providence, we mutually pledge to each other our Lives, our Fortunes and our sacred Honor.

Appendix

ALPHABETICAL LIST
OF THE
SIGNERS OF THE DECLARATION OF
INDEPENDENCE
AND THEIR BURIAL PLACES

Name	*State*	*Burial Place*
John Adams	Massachusetts	First Unitarian Church, Quincy, MA
Samuel Adams	Massachusetts	Old Granary Cemetery, Boston, MA
Josiah Bartlett	New Hampshire	Old Cemetery, Kingston, NH
Carter Braxton	Virginia	Burial place unknown
Charles Carroll of Carrollton	Maryland	Chapel of Doughregan Manor, Howard County, MD
Samuel Chase	Maryland	Old St. Paul's Cemetery, Baltimore, MD
Abraham Clark	New Jersey	Rahway Cemetery, Rahway, NJ
George Clymer	Pennsylvania	Friends Graveyard, Trenton, NJ
William Ellery	Rhode Island	Commons (Old City) Cemetery, Newport, RI
William Floyd	New York	Presbyterian Church Cemetery, Westernville, NY
Benjamin Franklin	Pennsylvania	Christ Church Cemetery, Philadelphia, PA
Elbridge Gerry	Massachusetts	Congressional Cemetery, Washington, DC
Button Gwinnett	Georgia	Colonial Cemetery, Savannah, GA

Name	State	Burial Place
Lyman Hall	Georgia	Signers Monument, Augusta, GA
John Hancock	Massachusetts	Old Granary Cemetery, Boston, MA
Benjamin Harrison	Virginia	Berkeley Plantation Family Cemetery, Charles City County, VA
John Hart	New Jersey	First Baptist Church Cemetery, Hopewell, NJ
Joseph Hewes	North Carolina	Christ Church Cemetery, Philadelphia, PA
Thomas Heyward, Jr.	South Carolina	Family Plantation, Old House, near Ridgeland, SC
William Hooper	North Carolina	Guilford Courthouse, National Military Park, Greensboro, NC
Stephen Hopkins	Rhode Island	North Burial Ground, Providence, RI
Francis Hopkinson	New Jersey	Christ Church Cemetery, Philadelphia, PA
Samuel Huntington	Connecticut	Norwich Town Cemetery Norwich, CT
Thomas Jefferson	Virginia	Monticello near Charlottesville, VA
Francis Lightfoot Lee	Virginia	Mount Airy Plantation, Richmond County, VA
Richard Henry Lee	Virginia	"Burnt House Fields" Family Plot, Westmoreland County, VA
Francis Lewis	New York	Trinity Churchyard, New York, NY
Philip Livingston	New York	Prospect Hill Cemetery, York, PA
Thomas Lynch, Jr.	South Carolina	Lost at sea
Thomas McKean	Delaware	Laurel Hill Cemetery, Philadelphia, PA
Arthur Middleton	South Carolina	Middleton Place near Charleston, SC

Name	State	Burial Place
Lewis Morris	New York	St. Ann's Episcopal Church, Bronx, NY
Robert Morris	Pennsylvania	Christ Church, Philadelphia, PA
John Morton	Pennsylvania	St.Paul's Cemetery, Chester, PA
Thomas Nelson, Jr.	Virginia	Grace Church, Yorktown, VA
William Paca	Maryland	Wye Plantation, Queen Anne's County, MD
Robert Treat Paine	Massachusetts	Old Granary Cemetery, Boston, MA
John Penn	North Carolina	Guilford Courthouse National Military Park, Greensboro, NC
George Read	Delaware	Immanuel Church, New Castle, DE
Caesar Rodney	Delaware	Christ Church, Dover, DE
George Ross	Pennsylvania	Christ Church Cemetery, Philadelphia, PA
Benjamin Rush	Pennsylvania	Christ Church Cemetery, Philadelphia, PA
Edward Rutledge	South Carolina	St. Philip's Church, Charleston, SC
Roger Sherman	Connecticut	Grove Street Cemetery, New Haven, CT
James Smith	Pennsylvania	First Presbyterian Church, York, PA
Richard Stockton	New Jersey	Friends Meeting House, Princeton, NJ
Thomas Stone	Maryland	"Habre de Venture" Plantation near La Plata, MD
George Taylor	Pennsylvania	Easton Cemetery, Easton, PA
Matthew Thornton	New Hampshire	Old Cemetery, Merrimack, NH

Name	State	Burial Place
George Walton	Georgia	Signers Monument, Augusta, GA
William Whipple	New Hampshire	North Cemetery, Portsmouth, NH
William Williams	Connecticut	Old Burying Ground, Lebanon, CT
James Wilson	Pennsylvania	Christ Church, Philadelphia, PA
John Witherspoon	New Jersey	Witherspoon Street Cemetery, Princeton, NJ
Oliver Wolcott	Connecticut	East Graveyard, Litchfield, CT
George Wythe	Virginia	St. John's Episcopal Church, Richmond, VA

THE CONGRESS IN 1776

Much momentum had been building toward the proclamation of a formal break with England, especially since Great Britain had issued the Coercive (Intolerable) Acts in 1774. These acts had closed the port of Boston, attempted to restrict the extent of self-government in Massachusetts, and provided for quartering British troops on the local citizenry. To make matters worse, General Thomas Gage was imposed on Massachusetts as a military governor. The climactic phase of the debate on separating from Great Britain occurred in Congress July 2-4, 1776. On the 2nd, Congress proclaimed American independence. For three days, however, Thomas Jefferson's draft of the Declaration of Independence was debated and revised. By the end of July 4, Congress had completed this process and produced the text that we know today.

Members Of Congress Present July 2-4, 1776

New Hampshire:	William Whipple, Josiah Bartlett.
Massachusetts:	John Hancock, John Adams, Samuel Adams, Elbridge Gerry, Robert Treat Paine.
Rhode Island:	Stephen Hopkins, William Ellery.
Connecticut:	Roger Sherman, Samuel Huntington.
New York:	George Clinton, William Floyd, Henry Wisner, Francis Lewis, John Alsop, Philip Livingston(?), Robert R. Livingston.
New Jersey:	Richard Stockton, John Witherspoon, Francis Hopkinson, Abraham Clark, John Hart.
Pennsylvania:	Benjamin Franklin, James Wilson, John Morton, John Dickinson, Robert Morris, Thomas Willing(?), Charles Humphreys(?).
Delaware:	Thomas McKean, George Read.
Maryland:	William Paca, Thomas Stone, John Rogers(?).
Virginia:	Thomas Jefferson, Benjamin Harrison, Thomas Nelson, Jr., Francis Lightfoot Lee, Carter Braxton.
North Carolina:	Joseph Hewes, John Penn.
South Carolina:	Edward Rutledge, Thomas Heyward, Jr., Thomas Lynch, Jr., Arthur Middleton, Thomas Lynch, Sr.(?).
Georgia:	Button Gwinnett, Lyman Hall, George Walton

Members Of Congress July-August 1776 Who Never Signed

Some members who were present during the debates of July 2-4, 1776 never signed the Declaration of Independence. In the listing below, an attempt is made to explain why they did not. It is, of course, clear that those not present in Congress on August 2, 1776 would not have been able to sign on that occasion. However, some who were absent then did sign later. Many who did not sign could indeed have done so. However, to many delegates, attendance at state constitutional conventions seemed far more important than attending sessions of the Continental Congress. Perhaps this is why the New York and Maryland state convention delegates did not, in most cases, bother to sign when they returned to Philadelphia. Some nonsigners, especially those from distant states like Georgia and South Carolina, never went back to Philadelphia again. It is easy for us to see now that these men missed their chance for immortality, but it was not obvious then that the Declaration of Independence would assume the place in history that it now occupies.

Connecticut:	Titus Hosmer was only an alternate at the time.
New York:	George Clinton was on military service.
	James Duane was at the New York Provincial Congress.
	John Jay was at the New York Provincial Congress.
	Robert R. Livingston was at the New York Provincial Congress.
	Philip Schuyler was on military service.
	Henry Wisner was at the New York Provincial Congress.
	John Alsop was at the New York Provincial Congress.
Pennsylvania:	Charles Humphreys was opposed to American independence.
	Thomas Mifflin was on military service.
	Thomas Willing opposed independence.
	John Dickinson opposed independence at that time.
Maryland:	Robert Alexander turned Loyalist after the Declaration was proclaimed.
	Thomas Johnson was at the Maryland Constitutional Convention.

	John Rogers was not returned to Congress and left Philadelphia about July 12.
	Matthew Tilghman was at the Maryland Constitutional Convention.
North Carolina:	Richard Caswell was on military service.
South Carolina:	Thomas Lynch, Sr. was extremely ill.
	Henry Middleton was chairing a committee to organize the state government of South Carolina.
	John Rutledge was President (governor) of South Carolina.
Georgia:	Archibald Bullock was President (governor) of Georgia.

Members Of Congress Who Signed But Were Absent July 2-4, 1776

Maryland:	Samuel Chase and Charles Carroll were attending the Maryland Constitutional Convention.
Virginia:	Richard Henry Lee returned home because of family illness.
	George Wythe was attending the Virginia Constitutional Convention.
North Carolina:	William Hooper arrived after July 4, apparently delayed by illness.

Those Who Signed After August 2, 1776

New Hampshire:	Matthew Thornton probably signed shortly after his arrival in Philadelphia in November.
Massachusetts:	Elbridge Gerry was away from Philadelphia from July 16 to September 9.
Connecticut:	Oliver Wolcott signed after he returned to Philadelphia in late September.
New York:	Lewis Morris probably signed in late September.
Delaware:	Thomas McKean stated that he signed sometime in 1781; his name is missing from the list of singers published in 1777.
Virginia:	Richard Henry Lee signed after August 27.
	George Wythe signed after September 23.

Signers Not Members Of Congress July 2-4, 1776

The following signers were elected after the debates on independence, and were allowed to sign when they arrived in Congress. The five Pennsylvania signers listed here were all elected to replace the delegates from that state who had refused to support independence when it was voted upon on July 2.

New Hampshire: Matthew Thornton.
Connecticut: William Williams.
Pennsylvania: Benjamin Rush, George Clymer, James Smith, George Taylor, George Ross.

Of this group, only Matthew Thornton signed after August 2. The others were all present for the general signing on that day.

The Committee To Prepare The Declaration Of Independence

The following committee was chosen on June 11, 1776, to draft the text of the Declaration of Independence. This is the document which Congress reviewed and revised July 2-4, 1776, after the Lee resolutions proclaiming independence from Great Britain had been approved.

Thomas Jefferson of Virginia was the actual author of the Declaration.

John Adams of Massachusetts, who insisted that Jefferson write the Declaration, provided only a few suggestions of his own. Adams believed that a declaration written by Jefferson, a Virginian and a skillful writer, would be more acceptable to Congress than one written by Adams, a New Englander, who had already alienated some of the other delegates by his acerbity and petulance.

Benjamin Franklin of Pennsylvania made only minor suggestions. The story goes that no one really wanted Franklin to do the actual writing lest he conceal a few jokes in the text. In fact, the shrewd Philadelphian recognized the hard reality that Adams's evaluation of the wisdom of letting Jefferson do the writing showed good judgment and was strategically sound.

Roger Sherman of Connecticut played no role in the preparation of the text. He too recognized that Jefferson was the proper man for that assignment.

Robert Livingston of New York played no part in preparing the text and never subsequently signed the document.

What Was The Problem For New York?

New York faced a unique problem when it came time to vote independence up or down. It alone, of all the thirteen states, had specific instructions not to vote on the question of separation from England. Other states had taken steps to free their delegates for such a vote, but not New York. For example, New Jersey had replaced three of its delegates who were cool toward independence, and replaced them with men whose favorable vote could be relied upon. After the July 2 vote on the Lee resolutions, Pennsylvania replaced its opponents of independence with supporters of the cause. Maryland lifted its restrictions just in time to enable its delegates to support the Lee resolutions. The other states left their delegates free to vote as they wished on the subject, although both Virginia and North Carolina sent instructions to their delegations urging them to support any move for independence that arose in Congress.

As late as June 11, 1776, the Third Provincial Congress of New York renewed the voting prohibition on its Congressional delegates. However, the Fourth Provincial Congress, which convened at White Plains on July 9, not only approved independence, but eventually incorporated the text of the Declaration into the first New York state constitution in 1777. The New York delegates were, therefore, free to support independence after July 9 and did so.

SOME PRELIMINARIES TO THE DECLARATION OF INDEPENDENCE

The Declaration of Independence did not spring spontaneously into existence without hints that it was coming. Several of the colonies, later to be states, had issued challenges of their own to British rule. A few of the more famous of these are listed below.

Suffolk Resolves: A committee of leaders of Suffolk County, Massachusetts, south of Boston, declared the Coercive Acts unconstitutional and not binding. This committee urged the citizens of the state to form their own government, collect their own taxes, and withhold revenues from the royal authorities until the Coercive Acts were repealed. This call, issued on September 9, 1774, was presented to the First

Continental Congress on September 18.

Mecklenburg Resolutions: A committee in Charlotte, Mecklenburg County, North Carolina, passed a set of resolutions that were once believed to be a call for independence. These resolutions were intended for the Second Continental Congress, but never presented to it. The original text seems to have disappeared, but an 1847 newspaper version contains no reference to independence or a "free and independent people." The date of the resolutions was May 31, 1775.

Halifax Resolves: The Fourth Provincial Congress of North Carolina, meeting in the small town of Halifax, authorized its state's Congressional delegates to "concur with the delegates of the other Colonies in declaring Independency." These resolves are dated April 12, 1776.

Virginia Resolutions: The Virginia Convention, called to establish a state government, not only authorized its delegates to agree to independence, it urged them to take the lead in formulating such a declaration. Approved May 5, 1776, the Virginia resolutions were transmitted to Congress, along with the Halifax Resolves, on May 27. Congress tabled them until June 7, when their essence was moved in Congress by Richard Henry Lee.

"Certain Resolutions Respecting Independency"

The following three resolutions were offered to Congress on June 7, 1776, by Richard Henry Lee of Virginia:

Resolved, That these United Colonies are, and of right ought to be, free and independent states, that they are absolved from all allegiance to the British Crown, and that all political connection between them and the State of Great Britain is, and ought to be, totally dissolved.

That it is expedient forthwith to take the most effectual measures for the forming of foreign Alliances.

That a plan of confederation be prepared and transmitted to the respective Colonies for their consideration and approbation.

BIBLIOGRAPHY

Becker, Carl. *The Declaration of Independence; A Study in the History of Political Ideas.* (New York: Knopf, 1956, reprint of 1922 original).

Boyd, Julian P. *The Declaration of Independence: the Evolution of the Text as Shown in Facsimiles of Various Drafts by Its Author.* (Washington: Library of Congress, 1943).

Burnett, Edmund C. *Letters of Members of the Continental Congress.* Vol. II. (Washington: Carnegie Institution, 1923).

Chidsey, Donald B. *July 4, 1776; the Dramatic Story of the First Four Days of July 1776.* (New York: Crown, 1958).

Donovan, Frank R. *Mr. Jefferson's Declaration.* (New York: Dodd, Mead, 1968).

Dumbauld, Edward. *The Declaration of Independence and What It Means Today.* (Norman: University of Oklahoma Press, 1950).

Friedenwald, Herbert. *The Declaration of Independence: an Interpretation and What It Means Today.* (New York: Da Capo Press, 1974, reprint of 1904 original).

Hawke, David F. *Honorable Treason; the Declaration of Independence and the Men Who Signed It.* (New York: Viking Press, 1976).

Malone, Dumas. *The Story of the Declaration of Independence.* (New York: Oxford University Press, 1954).

Michael, William H. *The Declaration of Independence; Illustrated Story of Its Adoption, with the Biographies and Portraits of the Signers.* (Washington: United States Government Printing Office. 1904).

National Park Service. *Signers of the Declaration of Independence; Historic Places Commemorating the Signing of the Declaration of Independence.* (Washington: United States Government Printing Office, 1974).

Sanderson, John. *Biography of the Signers to the Declaration of Independence.* Nine volumes. (Philadelphia: R. W. Pomeroy, 1823-1827).

PUBLICATIONS OF
THE BRONX COUNTY HISTORICAL SOCIETY

The Beautiful Bronx (1920-1950) by Lloyd Ultan

The Bronx in the Innocent Years (1890-1925) by Lloyd Ultan and
Gary Hermalyn

*The Bronx in Print: An Annotated Catalogue of Books and
Pamphlets about the Bronx* edited by Candace Khuta and
Narcisco Rodriquez

The Bronx Triangle: A Portrait of Norwood by Edna Mead

*Genealogy of The Bronx: An Annotated Guide to Sources of
Information* by Gary Hermalyn and Laura Tosi

History in Asphalt: The Origin of Bronx Street and Place Names
by John McNamara

History of the Morris Park Racecourse and the Morris Family
by Nicholas DiBrino

Legacy of The Revolution: The Valentine-Varian House
by Lloyd Ultan

*Morris High School and the Creation of the New York City Public
High School System* by Gary Hermalyn

*The South Bronx and the Founding of America:
An Activity Book for Teachers and Students* by Lisa Garrison

Edgar Allan Poe: A Short Biography by Kathleen A. McAuley

Poems of Edgar Allan Poe at Fordham by Elizabeth Beirne

Edgar Allan Poe at Fordham Teachers Guide
by   Kathleen A. McAuley

The Signers of the Constitution of the United States
by Brother C. Edward Quinn

The Signers of the Declaration of Independence
by Brother C. Edward Quinn

*Bicentennial of the United States Constitution Commemorative Issue
The Bronx County Historical Society Journal*

Periodicals

The Bronx County Historical Society Journal, published twice
a year since 1964.

The Bronx Historian: Newsletter

Eureka: Newsletter of the Friends of Edgar Allan Poe Cottage

Library News

EDGAR ALLAN POE COTTAGE

c. 1812

Poe Cottage is administered by The Bronx County Historical Society in agreement with the Department of Parks and Recreation of the City of New York

Guided Tours

POE PARK

*Grand Concourse & East Kingsbridge Road
The Bronx, New York 10467
Telephone: (212) 881-8900*

VALENTINE-VARIAN HOUSE

c. 1758

MUSEUM OF BRONX HISTORY

*The Valentine-Varian House, owned and administered by
The Bronx County Historical Society,
was donated by Mr. William C. Beller.*

*3266 Bainbridge Avenue at East 208th Street
The Bronx, New York 10467
Telephone: (212) 881-8900*

*The Bronx County Historical Society is supported
in part with public funds and services provided through
The Department of Cultural Affairs and
The Department of Parks and Recreation of The City of New York,
The Office of the President of the Borough of The Bronx,
The New York State Council on the Arts,
New York Council for the Humanities,
New York State Office of Parks, Recreation and Historic Preservation,
The New York State Library
and the Institute of Museum Services.*

THE BRONX COUNTY HISTORICAL SOCIETY

The Bronx County Historical Society was founded in 1955 for the purpose of promoting knowledge, interest and research in The Bronx. The Society administers The Museum of Bronx History, Edgar Allan Poe Cottage, a Research Library, and The Bronx County Archives; publishes a varied series of books, journals and newsletters; conducts historical tours, lectures, courses, school programs, archaeological digs and commemorations; designs exhibitions; sponsors various expeditions; and produces the "Out of the Past" radio show and cable television programs. The Society is active in furthering the arts, preserving the natural resources of The Bronx, and in creating the sense of pride in the Bronx Community.

For additional information, please contact:

THE BRONX COUNTY HISTORICAL SOCIETY
3309 Bainbridge Avenue, The Bronx, New York 10467
Telephone: (212) 881-8900

872884

920
Qui

Quinn, Bro. C. Edward
The Signers of the
Declaration of Indepen-
dence